HOME REPAIR AND IMPROVEMENT

PAINT AND WALLPAPER

TIME®
LIFE
BOOKS

Other Publications
THE TIME-LIFE COMPLETE GARDENER
JOURNEY THROUGH THE MIND AND BODY
WEIGHT WATCHERS® SMART CHOICE RECIPE COLLECTION
TRUE CRIME
THE AMERICAN INDIANS
THE ART OF WOODWORKING
LOST CIVILIZATIONS
ECHOES OF GLORY
THE NEW FACE OF WAR
HOW THINGS WORK
WINGS OF WAR
CREATIVE EVERYDAY COOKING
COLLECTOR'S LIBRARY OF THE UNKNOWN
CLASSICS OF WORLD WAR II
TIME-LIFE LIBRARY OF CURIOUS AND UNUSUAL FACTS
AMERICAN COUNTRY
VOYAGE THROUGH THE UNIVERSE
THE THIRD REICH
MYSTERIES OF THE UNKNOWN
TIME FRAME
FIX IT YOURSELF
FITNESS, HEALTH AND NUTRITION
SUCCESSFUL PARENTING
HEALTHY HOME COOKING
UNDERSTANDING COMPUTERS
LIBRARY OF NATIONS
THE ENCHANTED WORLD
THE KODAK LIBRARY OF CREATIVE PHOTOGRAPHY
GREAT MEALS IN MINUTES
THE CIVIL WAR
PLANET EARTH
COLLECTOR'S LIBRARY OF THE CIVIL WAR
THE EPIC OF FLIGHT
THE GOOD COOK
WORLD WAR II
THE OLD WEST

*For information on and a full description
of any of the Time-Life Books series listed above,
please call 1-800-621-7026 or write:*
Reader Information
Time-Life Customer Service
P.O. Box C-32068
Richmond, Virginia 23261-2068

PAINT AND WALLPAPER

BY THE EDITORS OF TIME-LIFE BOOKS, ALEXANDRIA, VIRGINIA

The Consultants

Jeff Palumbo is a registered journeyman carpenter who has a home-building and remodeling business in northern Virginia. His interest in carpentry was sparked by his grandfather, a master carpenter with more than 50 years' experience. Palumbo teaches in the Fairfax County Adult Education Program.

Mark M. Steele is a professional home inspector in the Washington, D.C., area. He has developed and conducted training programs in home-ownership skills for first-time homeowners. He appears frequently on television and radio as an expert in home repair and consumer topics.

CONTENTS

Painting Like a Pro—Inside

Fresh paint is an inexpensive and largely foolproof way to refurbish a home. Paint can transform a room, altering the sense of space, disguising faults, and dramatizing virtues. Every trade has its tricks, and painting is no exception. This chapter includes helpful techniques and procedures for preparing surfaces, choosing the right tools, and applying paint in the interior of your home.

The first strokes with a roller →

You will need at least one ladder to complete many painting and wallpapering jobs. The following pages describe the various types of ladders that are available and how to work safely with each.

Construction: Ladders are available in wood, aluminum, and fiberglass. Aluminum ladders offer several advantages. They are no more expensive than the other types, weigh about 20 percent less, and are durable and easy to maintain. Their major drawback, however, is that they conduct electricity. If you plan to work near electrical cables, purchase a wood or fiberglass ladder instead.

Strength: A ladder's rating number indicates its strength. Type IA is the strongest; it can bear loads up to 300 pounds. IA is followed, in order of decreasing strength, by Type I, Type II, and Type III, which can support 200 pounds. For added assurance, look for an "ANSI" seal, which means the ladder has been approved by the American National Standards Institute.

Platforms and Scaffolds: Ladders by themselves may be insufficient for certain jobs. Stairwells, for example, may be impossible to paint or paper without a platform like the one shown on page 10. Exterior painting, particularly with a sprayer (pages 66-67), is facilitated above level ground by using brackets called ladder jacks to support a platform of planks from two extension ladders (page 11). Use only specially fabricated planks that are available at scaffold- and ladder-rental stores. If your yard is uneven—or if the house structure prevents setting up the ladders within reach of the work—hire a professional to erect scaffolding.

Maintenance: Before climbing a ladder, inspect it for components that are cracked, twisted, jammed, or loose. If you find any defects, do not attempt repairs; get a new ladder. When you are not using the ladder, store it horizontally on at least three large, strong hooks in a dry place. To ensure smooth operation, periodically lubricate all its movable parts.

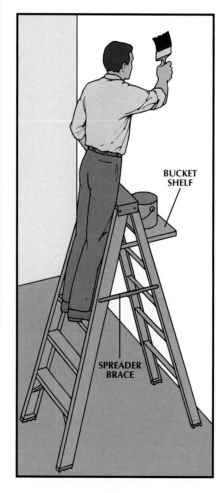

BUCKET SHELF

SPREADER BRACE

Some Ladder "Don'ts"

✔ Don't set up a ladder in front of a closed, unlocked door; either lock the door or open it.
✔ Don't level a ladder's feet by placing objects under them.
✔ Don't use a ladder in a high wind.
✔ Don't stand a ladder on ice, snow, or any other slippery surface.
✔ Don't lean the top of a ladder against a windowpane or screen.
✔ Don't link ladders to add height.
✔ Don't place a metal ladder near electrical wires.
✔ Don't step from one ladder to another.
✔ Don't carry tools in your hands or pockets while climbing. Set them on the shelf of a stepladder; if you are working on an extension ladder, place them in a bucket and hoist them up with a rope.
✔ Don't hold a paint bucket with one hand while painting. Instead, place it on the shelf of a stepladder or hang it from a rung of an extension ladder with a hook.
✔ Don't stand above the third-highest rung of an extension ladder or the second-highest step of a stepladder.
✔ Don't overreach to either side of the ladder.
✔ Don't take both hands off the ladder at once.

The versatile stepladder.
◆ Open the ladder to its fullest extent, lock its spreader braces into place, and push the bucket shelf down as far as it will go.
◆ Place the four legs on level ground or a level floor.
◆ Mount the ladder one step at a time, always facing the ladder and holding onto upper steps—not the side rails—with both hands as you climb.

Setting up an extension ladder.

◆ Place the ladder flat on the ground, with its feet a few inches from the vertical surface to be painted.

◆ Raise the top end. Then, grasping the rungs hand over hand, "walk" the ladder to a vertical position *(right)*.

◆ Lift the bottom slightly and shift the ladder outward so it leans firmly against the wall. You can compensate for uneven ground with leg levelers *(page 10)*.

The Right Angle for a Ladder

Use the following technique to set an extension ladder against a wall at a safe angle. After raising the ladder, move the base away from the wall so that your outstretched arms comfortably reach the rung nearest to shoulder height when you stand with your toes touching the ladder feet *(right)*.

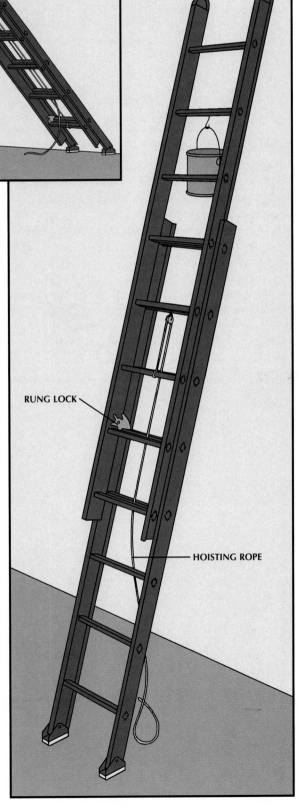

RUNG LOCK

HOISTING ROPE

Extending the ladder.

◆ Pull the hoisting rope to raise the upper section to the desired height. Check to see that the rung locks on the upper section have fully engaged against the rungs on the lower section.

◆ Set the ladder at a safe angle against the wall using the procedure that is described above.

⚠️ *Make sure the upper section overlaps the lower one by at*
CAUTION *least 3 feet.*

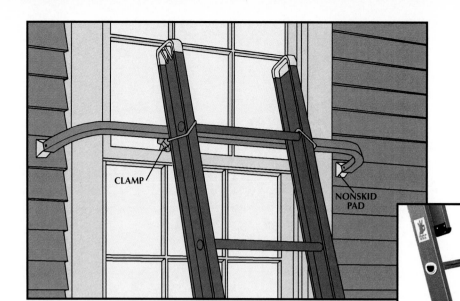

CLAMP

NONSKID PAD

Ladder accessories.

A ladder stabilizer *(above)* provides a broad, sturdy base for the top of an extension ladder. It also lifts the ladder away from the wall to provide easier access to roof overhangs. Stabilizers are available in a variety of materials and designs; the one shown above is made of square aluminum tubing bent into a shallow U that is wide enough to bridge a window. The stabilizer clamps to the ladder rails at the highest rung, and has nonskid pads that prevent the ladder from slipping or marring the wall.

Leg levelers *(photograph)* allow you to set a ladder on uneven surfaces. Fasten one to each rail of the ladder according to the manufacturer's instructions, then adjust them independently to make the rungs level.

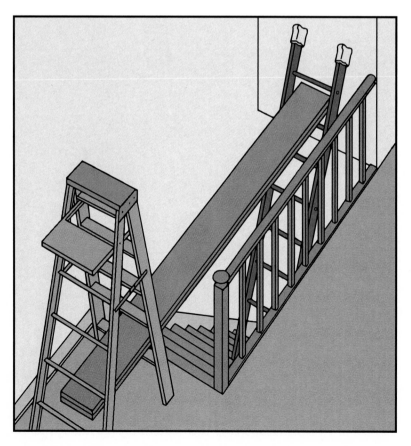

A platform for a stairwell.

To paint the ceiling and walls above a staircase, fashion a platform from a straight ladder, a stepladder, and scaffold planks. Protect the wall above the stairwell by fitting the ladder rails with foam-rubber protectors.

◆ Place the straight ladder on the staircase and lean it against the wall as shown on page 9.
◆ Set the stepladder at the top of the stairs.
◆ Lay the planking on a lower rung of the stepladder and on whichever rung of the straight ladder makes the planks level, or nearly so.

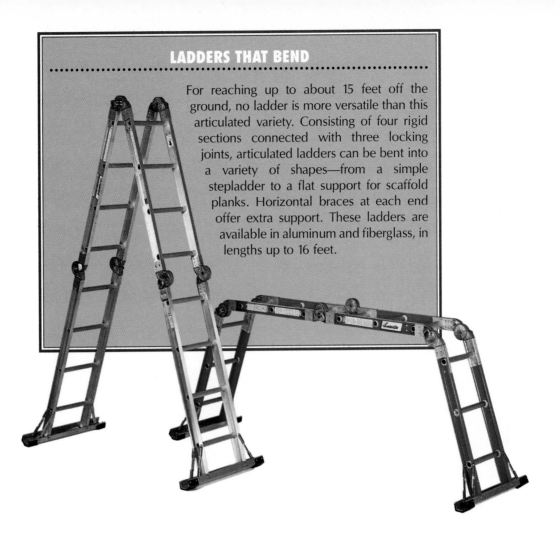

LADDERS THAT BEND

For reaching up to about 15 feet off the ground, no ladder is more versatile than this articulated variety. Consisting of four rigid sections connected with three locking joints, articulated ladders can be bent into a variety of shapes—from a simple stepladder to a flat support for scaffold planks. Horizontal braces at each end offer extra support. These ladders are available in aluminum and fiberglass, in lengths up to 16 feet.

Turning ladders into scaffolding.
Two Type I or IA extension ladders, two 2-by-10 scaffold planks 10 feet long, and a pair of ladder jacks like those at right are the ingredients for this one-person painting scaffold.

◆ Adjust the lengths of the ladders so that the rung at the height you wish to stand—no more than 20 feet—will lie about $2\frac{1}{2}$ feet from the wall ($3\frac{1}{2}$ feet for spraying).

◆ Lean the ladders against the wall no more than 8 feet apart and attach the ladder jacks to the rungs *(right)* or rails, depending on the model. Level the arm of each jack with its brace.

◆ With a helper, carry the planks one at a time up the ladders and lay them across the arms of the ladder jacks.

⚠ **CAUTION** *Be careful when working from this kind of platform; there are no handholds or safety rails to keep you from falling.*

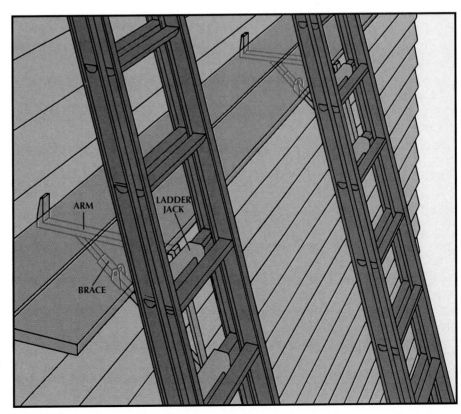

ARM

LADDER JACK

BRACE

Tool Kit for Interior Work

Like most jobs, painting requires a variety of tools and materials. General-purpose items—such as a hammer, a screwdriver, a sturdy knife, a can opener, and masking tape—you probably already have on hand. For cleaning up, you'll need rags and metal containers such as coffee cans or loaf pans.

You may, however, need to purchase many of the tools that are shown here, as well as other items. Buy drop cloths to protect both furniture and floors from paint drips and spatters. You'll also need a sanding block and several grades of sandpaper to smooth repairs to walls and woodwork, and a sponge to clean up dust and dirt and to wash down previously painted walls. As an auxiliary container for paint, a medium-size rustproof pail is ideal.

Appropriate protective gear includes rubber gloves, goggles, and a dust mask. A respirator may be necessary with a few toxic paint removers.

CAULKING GUN

6" PUTTY KNIFE

3" PUTTY KNIFE

1¼" PUTTY KNIFE

Tools for repairing surfaces.
For patching wallboard, plaster, and trim before painting, you will need both stiff- and flexible-blade putty knives, and a wide-blade putty knife for taping wallboard. Extensive filling of joints around trim and baseboards requires a caulking gun.

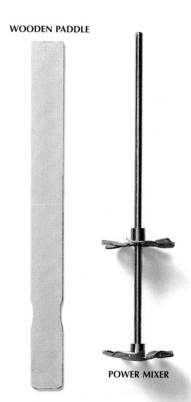

WOODEN PADDLE

POWER MIXER

Mixing tools.
Paint must be stirred thoroughly to cover surfaces evenly. For small quantities, wooden paddles are satisfactory, but a power mixer driven by an electric drill works faster, especially when blending large quantities.

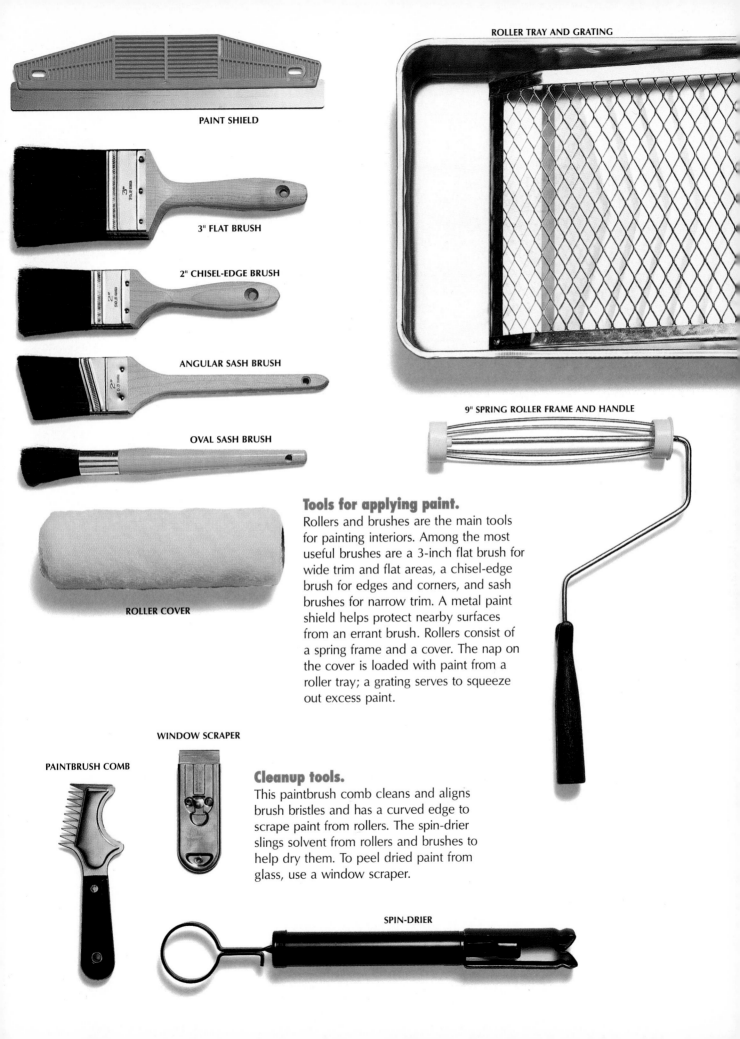

PAINT SHIELD

3" FLAT BRUSH

2" CHISEL-EDGE BRUSH

ANGULAR SASH BRUSH

OVAL SASH BRUSH

ROLLER COVER

ROLLER TRAY AND GRATING

9" SPRING ROLLER FRAME AND HANDLE

Tools for applying paint.
Rollers and brushes are the main tools
for painting interiors. Among the most
useful brushes are a 3-inch flat brush for
wide trim and flat areas, a chisel-edge
brush for edges and corners, and sash
brushes for narrow trim. A metal paint
shield helps protect nearby surfaces
from an errant brush. Rollers consist of
a spring frame and a cover. The nap on
the cover is loaded with paint from a
roller tray; a grating serves to squeeze
out excess paint.

WINDOW SCRAPER

PAINTBRUSH COMB

Cleanup tools.
This paintbrush comb cleans and aligns
brush bristles and has a curved edge to
scrape paint from rollers. The spin-drier
slings solvent from rollers and brushes to
help dry them. To peel dried paint from
glass, use a window scraper.

SPIN-DRIER

The durability of any paint job depends largely on the care with which you have prepared the surfaces before you apply the paint.

For virgin wallboard, plaster, or wood, first dust the surface thoroughly, then brush a coat of primer on surfaces that you plan to paint *(pages 118-121)*.

If you are working with finished surfaces, try to ascertain whether the material beneath the finish is wallboard or plaster, and the type of surface covering that was used *(pages 116-121)*. Such information will determine how you proceed with preparation treatments and will help you to select the proper undercoatings, primers, and paints. Next, inspect the room thoroughly for damage that may call for repairs.

Dealing with Old Paint: Check for blistering, cracking, or peeling paint and scrape it off *(pages 16-17)* or remove it with a nylon paint stripper that is fitted to an electric drill. If it is necessary for you to remove many layers of paint, consider using a heat gun *(page 55)*. When the damaged paint is near window glass, strip it with a chemical paint remover rather than risk breaking the glass with a power tool *(page 17)*.

Concealing Flaws: Repair damaged wallboard or plaster *(pages 20-27)*, and fill in gouges, holes, and cracks in walls and trim. When choosing a filler, read the label to be sure the product is compatible with the finish you plan to use.

Build up depressions and conceal nails with spackling compound. Use the same material to repair short open joints; longer gaps—along a baseboard, for example—are better caulked than patched with spackling compound.

On surfaces that are bare and those that have been painted, follow repair work with a thorough sanding. Electric sanders speed the work, but for small areas, a sanding block works well *(opposite)*.

Special Surfaces: New paint will not adhere properly to glossy surfaces; dull such finishes by raising a nap with sandpaper or a liquid deglosser. Strip off wallpaper *(pages 72-75)* or prepare it for painting *(page 19)*. If floor wax has adhered to baseboards, take it off with wax remover. Brush rust from radiators, pipes, and heat ducts *(page 59)*, and clean mildew from damp places *(page 53)*. Interior brick *(page 60)* and garage and basement surfaces *(page 61)* require special preparations.

Cleaning: Dirt, grease, and even fingerprints can prevent new paint from adhering firmly. A good washing down with a heavy-duty household detergent just before painting will usually suffice for finished walls and woodwork. Finally, be sure that surfaces are completely dry before painting.

⚠ **CAUTION** *Paint strippers, solvents, and cleaning agents can give off harmful fumes. Follow the advice on page 29.*

TOOLS

Putty knives (flexible- and stiff-blade)
Inexpensive paint-brush
Sharp knife
Long-nose pliers
Nail set
Hammer

MATERIALS

Sandpaper (fine- and medium-grit)
Spackling compound
Wood putty
Wood filler
Primer
Paint remover

Paint solvent
Shellac
Caulk
Wallpaper primer-sealer

SAFETY TIPS

Protect your hands from cleaning agents and paint solvents. Wear rubber gloves and goggles to apply paint remover, and add a respirator if the product contains methylene chloride. When sanding, wear a dust mask.

Safety Measures for Lead and Asbestos

Lead and asbestos, known health hazards, pervade houses constructed, remodeled, or redecorated before 1978. Test all painted surfaces for lead with a kit, available at hardware stores, or call your local health department or environmental protection office for other options. Asbestos was once a component of wallboard, joint compound, acoustic or decorative ceiling and wall materials, duct insulation, and heatproofing materials. Mist such materials with a solution of 1 teaspoon low-sudsing detergent per quart of water to suppress dust, then remove small samples for testing by a National Institute of Standards and Technology-certified lab.

Paint preparation where lead or asbestos is present requires a tightly fitting respirator and protective clothing that's hot to wear. Hire a professional licensed in hazardous-substance removal if you suffer from cardiac or respiratory problems or don't tolerate heat well. And hire a professional for indoor jobs that require disturbing large areas of these materials.

When working with hazardous materials, take the following precautions:

! Keep children, pregnant women, and pets out of the work area.

! Indoors, seal off the work area from the rest of the house with 6-mil polyethylene sheeting and duct tape and turn off air conditioning and forced-air heating systems. Cover rugs and furniture that can't be removed with more sheeting and tape.

! Wear protective clothing (available from a safety equipment supply house or paint store) and a dual-cartridge respirator with high efficiency particulate air (HEPA) filters.

! If you must use a power sander on paint containing lead, get one equipped with a HEPA-filter vacuum, but never sand asbestos-laden materials or cut them with power machinery. Mist them with water and detergent, and remove with a hand tool.

! Avoid tracking dust from the work area into other parts of the house, and take off protective clothing (including shoes) before leaving the work area. Shower and wash hair immediately. Wash clothing separately.

! When you finish indoor work, mop the area twice, then run a vacuum cleaner equipped with a HEPA filter. Dispose of materials as recommended by your local health department or environmental protection office.

SANDING TECHNIQUES

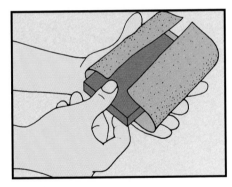

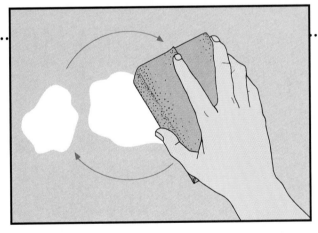

1. Making a sanding block.
You can buy a ready-made sanding block, but a homemade one works just as well.
◆ From a scrap of 1-by-3 or 1-by-4 board, cut a block 4 or 5 inches long.
◆ Cut a rectangle of sandpaper large enough to encircle the block. For previously painted surfaces, start with medium-grit sandpaper then proceed to fine-grit paper; for virgin wood, use only fine-grit paper.
◆ Wrap the paper around the block with the grit side out.

2. Sanding flat areas.
◆ Make sure that all loose paint is removed from the area to be sanded *(pages 16-17)* and that any patching compounds are completely dry.
◆ Grasp the block firmly, holding the sandpaper snugly around it.
◆ On a painted surface, sand with a gentle, circular motion, and feather the edges of the area by blending the old paint or patching materials into the surrounding surface; on bare wood, work in straight strokes along the grain.
◆ Tap the sandpaper frequently on a hard surface to remove accumulated residue, and replace the paper when it becomes clogged or worn out.

A sanding edge for intricate jobs.

◆ Fold a 6-inch square of sandpaper into quarters to make a sharp sanding edge *(above, left)*.

◆ Place the edge against the surface to be sanded *(above, right)*, and gently rub the paper over the surface to blend the edges of patching material or old paint with the surrounding surface.

◆ Refold the paper as necessary to make fresh edges.

REPAIRING FLAWS IN PAINT

Scraping paint.

Insert the edge of a $1\frac{1}{4}$-inch-wide putty knife under the loose paint *(left)*, and being careful not to gouge the surface, scrape with a pushing motion. For large areas, use the scraper that is shown on page 55.

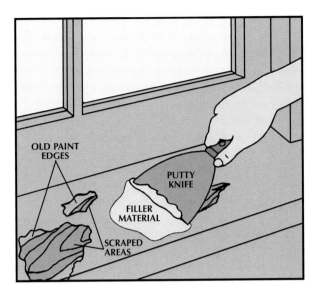

Filling in depressions.

◆ Apply spackling compound to a small depression with a flexible-blade putty knife; use a wide-blade putty knife for extensive filling.

◆ When the filler has dried, sand it flush with the surface.

◆ Spot-prime all scraped or filled areas before repainting *(pages 118-121)*.

STRIPPING OLD PAINT

1. Applying paint remover.

On most surfaces, a paste-type, water-base remover is safest. However, water in the paint remover may lift or buckle a wood veneer; use a solvent-base remover instead.

◆ Protect the surrounding area with a thick layer of newspaper.

◆ With a clean, inexpensive paintbrush, spread a generous amount of remover on the area to be stripped. Work with short strokes, brushing in one direction, and do not cover an area more than 2 feet square at one time.

2. Scraping off the paint.

◆ When the paint begins to blister and wrinkle, peel it off with a putty knife.

◆ As you remove the paint, clean the knife frequently with newspaper.

◆ When all paint is off, clean the bare surface using a wash of water or solvent as the label directs.

◆ Wait for the surface to dry, then smooth it lightly with fine-grit sandpaper.

TENDING TO WOOD KNOTS

Preparing the surface.
◆ Scrape off any hardened resin with a sharp paring knife or similar utensil and clean the area with turpentine.
◆ If the knot is loose, remove it with long-nose pliers and fill the hole with wood putty or wood filler.

To conceal a protruding knot that you cannot remove, build up the surrounding area with putty or filler and sand to an unobtrusive slope.

Sealing a knot.
◆ Sand the surface lightly, then paint it with thinned shellac.
◆ When the shellac is dry, sand the surface lightly once more.

TRIM AND MOLDING

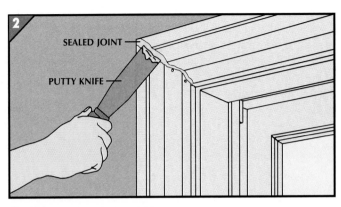

2. Filling a hole or joint.
With a flexible-blade putty knife, fill the nail holes with spackling compound or wood putty, depending on the surface you are preparing *(page 14).*

◆ For slightly opened joints around window frames and doorframes *(above),* apply spackling compound or wood putty, roughly shaping it to match the molding contours if the gap is wide. Caulk longer joints *(pages 56-57).*
◆ After the filler dries, check it for shrinkage and add more if needed.
◆ Sand the dried patches with fine-grit sandpaper.

1. Countersinking a nail.
◆ Place a nail set on the popped nailhead, with the shaft perpendicular to the surface *(above).*
◆ Strike the set with a hammer to embed the head about $\frac{1}{8}$ inch below the surface.

PAINTING OVER WALLPAPER

There are a number of sound reasons for stripping off wallpaper before painting *(pages 72-75).* Painstaking preparation counters most of them, but not all. For example, the design of a textured paper may show through the paint. And if you paint over several layers of paper, the combined weight of the layers and the paint may cause the paper to fall off the wall.

If you decide to paint a wallpapered surface, observe these principles: the paper must adhere firmly to the wall, it must be clean and grease free *(page 113),* any imperfections in the paper must be repaired *(pages 110-113),* and the surface must be treated with a wallpaper primer-sealer.

To patch an area of torn or missing wallpaper, first glue down any loose edges. Then cover the area with two thin layers of spackling compound, letting it dry between layers.

Apply the material with a wide-blade putty knife, extending the compound slightly beyond the edge of the damaged area. When the second layer is dry, sand the patch so that it is flush with the surrounding wallpaper.

If you wish to disguise a wallpapered surface, sand down the seams, then use the technique above to conceal them with spackling compound. Next, gently sand the entire surface of the wallpaper. Doing so raises a slight nap on the surface, so it will look less like painted-over wallpaper when the work is finished.

Vinyl- or plastic-coated paper will not hold paint, and wallpaper dyes may bleed through. Paint also can soften the adhesive holding the paper to the wall. To overcome these obstacles, coat all types of wallpaper with a wallpaper primer-sealer before painting.

Making Old Walls As Smooth As New

Before painting a room, you must correct all defects in walls and ceilings. Explained here and on the following pages are repair techniques both for wallboard (nowadays the standard building material) and for plaster on wood or metal lath.

Wallboard Repairs: Although builders now use screws to fasten wallboard to studs and joists, at one time they attached it with nails, which can pull away and protrude over time. Any such "popped" nail must be reseated and covered *(below and opposite)*.

Sometimes the taped seams between wallboard panels open up because of temperature changes or settling of a house. The gap can be closed with conventional paper tape or, in a step-saving method, with a fiberglass-mesh tape *(box, page 22)*.

Tactics for dealing with holes depend on the scale of the damage. You can fill in nail holes simply by covering them with ready-mixed vinyl spackling compound. For holes up to an inch across, stuff a wad of newspaper into the hole to give the compound something to adhere to. Larger holes—up to 6

inches across—require the more substantial backing of wire screening fastened to the inside of the wallboard *(page 23)*.

Patching Faults in Plaster: The basic strategy for plaster repairs is to clear away the damaged plaster, fill in the hole or crack, and sand the patch flush with the wall. For secure bonding of the patching material, large holes must be undercut *(page 26)*. All plaster patches are topped with a layer of spackling or wallboard joint compound, which are easier to sand than is plaster.

 TOOLS

Hammer
Putty knives
Sanding block
Finishing knife (10")
Scissors
Can opener

 MATERIALS

Nails
Wallboard joint
  compound
Sandpaper (fine-grit)
Wallboard joint tape
Wire screening
String
Patching plaster

SAFETY TIPS

Safety goggles protect your eyes when you are hammering. To keep from inhaling dust while sanding, wear a cartridge-type respirator.

RESEATING POPPED NAILS

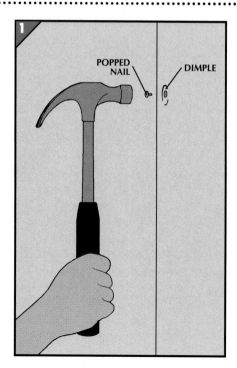

POPPED NAIL   DIMPLE

1. Securing and dimpling the nail.
Hammer the nail flush with the wallboard. Then carefully drive the nail a fraction of an inch below the surface, so the hammer's face creates a small depression, or dimple, in the surrounding wallboard without breaking the surface. (A driven and dimpled nail is shown to the right of the joint here.)

If the nail refuses to stay put, insert a new nail 2 inches directly above or below it. Dimple the new nail, then reseat the original one.

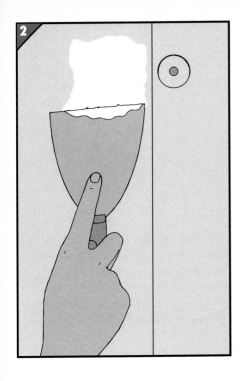

2. Patching the dimples.

◆ Apply a thin, smooth layer of joint compound over each dimple with a putty knife *(left)*. Let the compound dry; as it does, its color will change from dark to light beige.

◆ Apply a second layer of joint compound over a slightly larger area than the first layer.

◆ Smooth out any rough spots, especially at the edges, and let the patch dry.

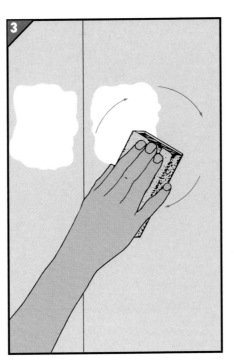

3. Leveling the surface.

◆ Gently sand the patches with fine-grit sandpaper wrapped around a sanding block. For smoothest results, rub the block across the patch in a circular motion.

◆ Feather the edges of the patches *(page 15)*, and clear away the dust before repainting.

RETAPING WALLBOARD JOINTS

1. Filling the joints.

◆ Remove any loose or damaged tape and crumbled joint compound from between the sections of wallboard.

◆ Spread a $\frac{1}{8}$-inch-thick layer of joint compound directly over the joint with a 6-inch-wide putty knife, pressing the knife firmly against the wallboard to force the compound into the joint.

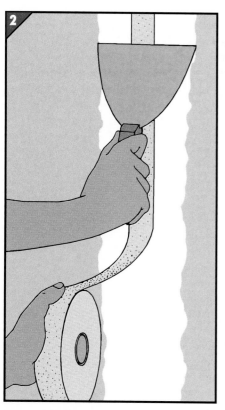

3. Covering the tape.
◆ Apply a thin, smooth layer of joint compound over the tape *(left)*. Use enough compound to extend this second layer about an inch beyond the edges of the layer applied in Step 1.
◆ Let the patch dry completely. Unless the weather is humid, this should take about 24 hours.

2. Applying the tape.
Before the joint compound dries, cover the filled seam with a single, unbroken piece of joint tape as follows:
◆ Roll out a 2-foot section of perforated paper joint tape.
◆ Center the end of the tape over the top of the joint, and press it into the joint compound.
◆ With the tape in one hand and the knife in the other, draw the knife over the tape at a 45-degree angle to embed it in the joint compound *(above)*. Unroll more tape in 2-foot sections as needed. If the tape wrinkles or veers away from the joint, lift it up carefully and recenter it.
◆ At the end of the seam, cut the tape from the roll.

When repairing only a short section of a joint, slightly overlap the ends of the old tape with the new tape.

A QUICKER JOINT WITH FIBERGLASS TAPE
··
Although perforated paper tape is the traditional material for covering wallboard joints, you can save some time by using fiberglass-mesh tape instead. Because this product is sticky on one side, you do not have to first apply joint compound to the seam for attachment. Simply stretch the mesh tape along the joint, pressing it down so that it adheres, then follow Steps 3 and 4 to finish the seam.

FIBERGLASS-MESH TAPE

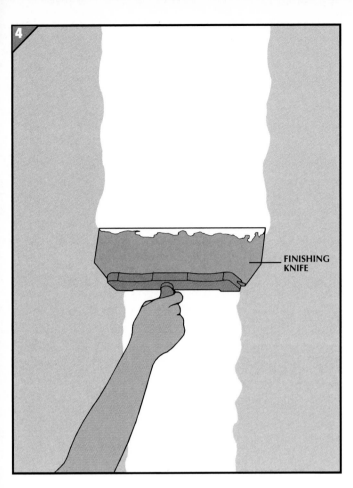

4. Applying the final coat.
This completion of the repair goes fastest if you use a 10-inch finishing knife instead of the 6-inch putty knife.
◆ Smooth on a very thin finish coat of joint compound in a layer about 10 to 12 inches wide.
◆ Let the patch dry.
◆ Sand the area with fine-grit sandpaper wrapped around a sanding block, feathering the edges *(page 15)*.

FINISHING KNIFE

FILLING HOLES IN WALLBOARD

1. Patching large holes.
◆ Remove the loose or torn wallboard around the opening.
◆ Cut a piece of wire screening that is slightly larger than the hole. Thread a length of string through the middle of the screen.
◆ Wet the inside edges of the hole with water and apply patching plaster to them. Then spread plaster on the inside of the wallboard, around the hole edge.
◆ Insert the screen through the hole *(right).* Pulling the ends of the string gently, draw the screening flat against the inside of the hole and embed it in the fresh plaster.

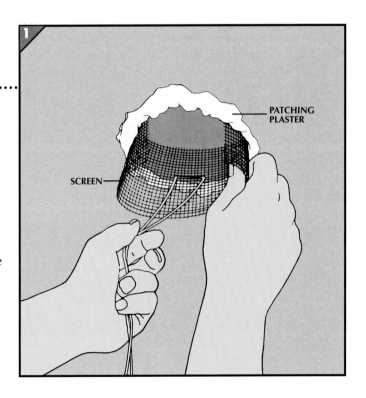

PATCHING PLASTER

SCREEN

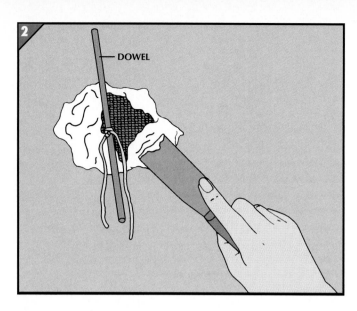

2. Initial filling.

◆ Secure the screen by placing a dowel across the opening and tying the ends of the string firmly around it.

◆ Fill the hole with plaster to a level almost—but not quite—flush with the wallboard surface *(left)*. Leave only a small gap around the string.

◆ Turn the dowel slightly to increase tension on the string and screen.

◆ Let the plaster set for 30 minutes.

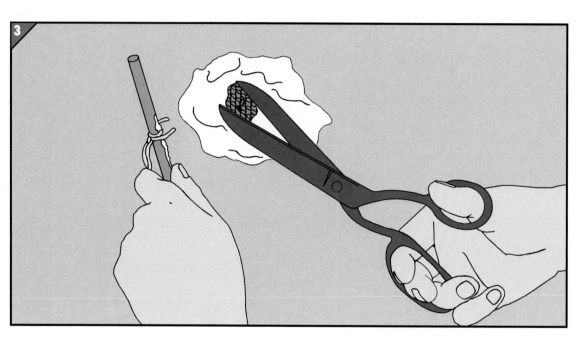

3. Removing the dowel.

◆ Cut the string as close to the screen as possible and then remove the dowel *(above)*.

◆ Wet the edges of the remaining gap and fill the gap with fresh plaster.

◆ Plaster over the entire patch to bring it flush with the wallboard surface.

◆ Allow the patch to set.

4. Final sealing.

◆ With a wide-blade putty knife, spread joint or spackling compound over the patch. Extend this final layer beyond the edges of the previous layer with long, smooth sweeps of the knife.

◆ Let the patch dry for about 24 hours.

◆ Finally, sand the patch with fine-grit sandpaper wrapped around a sanding block. Feather the edges of the patch *(page 15)*.

REPAIRING A HAIRLINE CRACK IN PLASTER

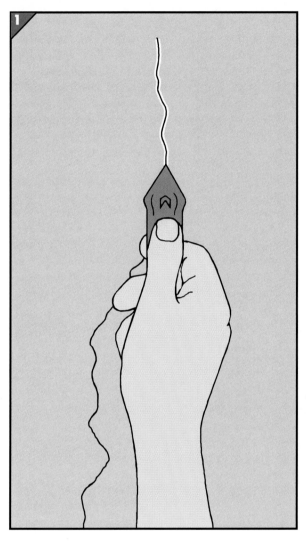

1. Cleaning.
◆ With the tip of a can opener, clear away loose plaster along the edges of the crack *(left)* so that the patching material will have a sound surface to grip.
◆ Remove a bit of the firm plaster at each end of the crack. This will keep the crack from extending farther in the future.
◆ Clear all dust out of the crack.

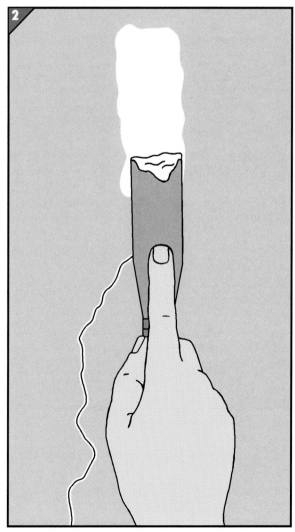

2. Sealing.
◆ Wet the crack and the surrounding area.
◆ Spread joint or spackling compound along the entire length of the crack. Make sure the patching material fills the crack completely and overlaps the solid edges.
◆ Let the patch dry for a day or so. If it shrinks, add another layer and allow it to dry.
◆ Sand the patch smooth.

PATCHING A HOLE IN PLASTER

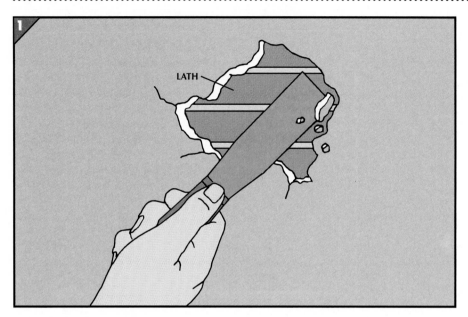

LATH

1. Preparation.
With a putty knife, clear away any loose or crumbling plaster from the edges of the hole, leaving sound plaster all around. If this enlarges the hole to more than 6 inches across, or if you find damaged lath underneath the plaster, call in a professional to complete the repair.

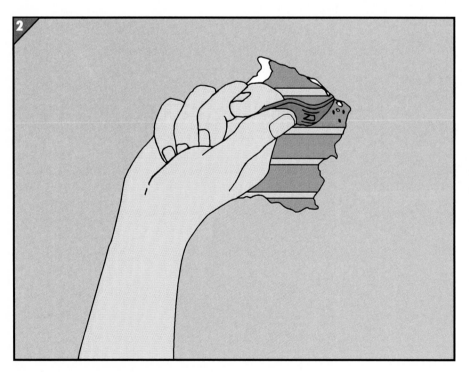

2. Undercutting.
◆ Using a can opener, undercut the edges to make the hole wider at the lath than it is at the surface *(left)*.
◆ Clear the plaster dust from the hole.

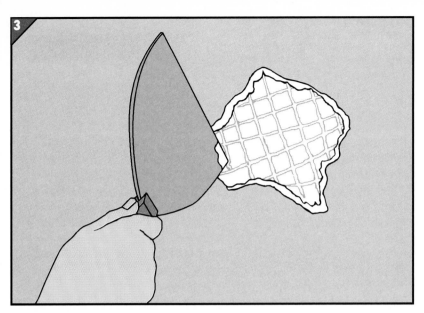

3. Applying the first layer.

◆ Moisten the edges of the hole and, if it is made of wood, the lath.

◆ Apply patching plaster to the edges, then fill the rest of the hole with plaster to about $\frac{1}{4}$ inch below the surface.

◆ While the plaster is still wet, score its surface *(left)*. The scoring will provide a better gripping surface for the next layer of plaster.

◆ Let the plaster set for 30 minutes.

4. Applying the second layer.

◆ Dampen the scored layer and 2 or 3 inches of undamaged surface around the hole.

◆ Fill the hole to the surface with plaster, spreading it an inch or so beyond the hole's edges.

◆ Draw the knife blade evenly over the patched area to smooth it.

◆ Let the plaster set.

5. Completing the patch.

◆ Cover the filled hole with a smooth layer of joint or spackling compound *(right)*. Spread the material an inch or so beyond the edges of the patching plaster.

◆ Let the patch dry for several days.

◆ Sand the area smooth and feather the edges of the patch into the surrounding surface *(page 15)*.

Thoroughly preparing a room before you paint is well worth the time and effort. Doing so not only shields room contents from the inevitable splattering of paint, but saves time when cleaning up and results in a neater job. The only tool you'll need is a screwdriver.

Begin by shifting furniture into the middle of the room and covering it with drop cloths. Cover the floor as well, taping newspaper along the baseboards. Newspaper also makes an excellent shield for radiators and other objects that can't be removed.

Electrical: Turn off the circuit breakers or unscrew the fuses for the room. Unscrew switch plates and receptacle covers *(page 106),* tape the screws to the plates, and set them near their original positions. If you wish, you can write the new paint brand, color, and type on a piece of masking tape and stick it to the back of one of the plates for future reference.

Loosen screws that secure light fixtures so that they stand away from the surface, allowing you to paint behind them later with a brush *(pages 34-35).* Tape plastic around the fixtures, and make sure not to turn them on while the plastic is in place.

Smooth away ridges of old paint around the openings with sandpaper, taking care to observe the precautions for dealing with lead and asbestos that are outlined on page 15. Turn the electricity back on for illumination if it is necessary, but exercise caution when painting around the openings.

Hardware: Uninterrupted surfaces are easier to paint than those with obstructions, so remove as much hardware as possible—unless, of course, the objects themselves are to be painted. You may wish to take off items such as window-sash locks, strike plates, and cabinet handles. Masking tape will protect parts that are not easily removed, such as hinges, locks, and thermostats. Doorknobs can be removed or masked.

Window Glass: Many painters use the technique called beading, which is shown on page 35, for window sashes and dividers, but you might wish to protect the glass instead. Run masking tape around the edges of the panes, leaving a $\frac{1}{16}$-inch gap between the edge of the tape and the wood or metal so that paint can form a seal on the glass. This will prevent condensation from damaging the frame. When you are finished painting, peel the tape away.

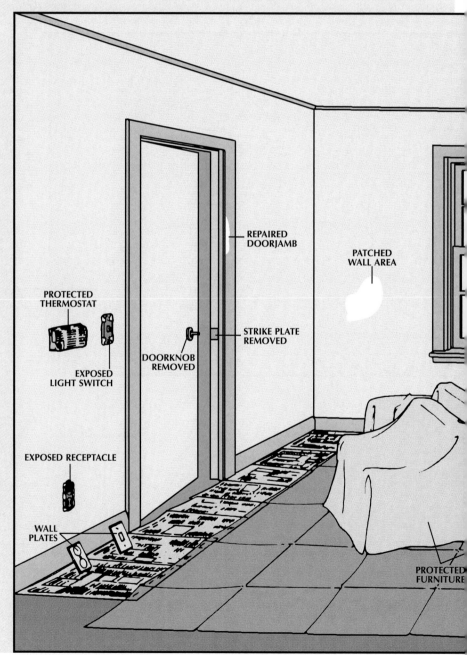

REPAIRED
DOORJAMB

PATCHED
WALL AREA

PROTECTED
THERMOSTAT

STRIKE PLATE
REMOVED

DOORKNOB
REMOVED

EXPOSED
LIGHT SWITCH

EXPOSED RECEPTACLE

WALL
PLATES

PROTECTED
FURNITURE

MATERIALS

Drop cloths	Sandpaper
Newspaper	Rags
Masking tape	
Plastic sheets	

Preparing a room for painting.

The illustration below indicates the wide range of repairs and preparation that may be required before painting begins. Most repairs, such as patching cracks and holes or sealing wood joints *(pages 14-27)*, will be necessary only from time to time.

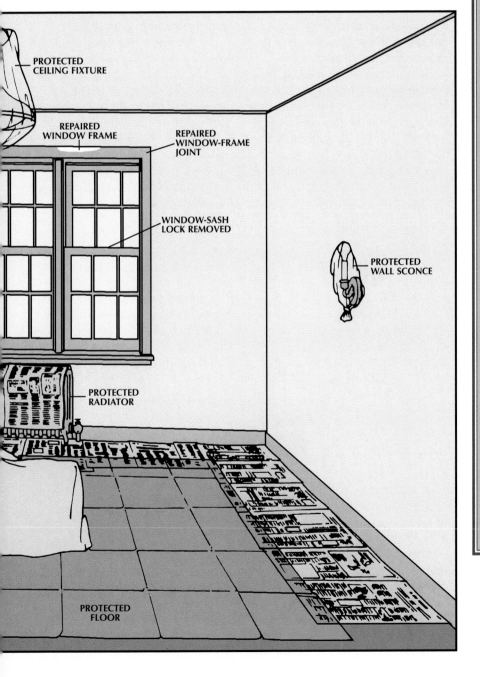

PROTECTED
CEILING FIXTURE

REPAIRED
WINDOW FRAME

REPAIRED
WINDOW-FRAME
JOINT

WINDOW-SASH
LOCK REMOVED

PROTECTED
WALL SCONCE

PROTECTED
RADIATOR

PROTECTED
FLOOR

Painting the Safe Way

Many products used in painting are toxic. Water-base products, such as latex paint, are the safest, but like most chemicals they contain poisonous ingredients. Use special care in handling solvent-base coatings such as alkyd paints, as well as related products like thinners, varnishes, and strippers. The fumes of some are so toxic that you may need a respirator approved by the National Institute of Occupational Safety and Health. Many of these products are highly flammable—some even require that you extinguish gas range or water-heater pilot lights before beginning work. In addition, follow these precautions:

✔ Keep children and pets out of the work area.

✔ Read labels of products for special requirements, and keep the labels on hand should you need to call a doctor.

✔ Work only in a ventilated room. Open doors and windows, and use fans to dispel fumes.

✔ When painting a ceiling, work in a position that prevents paint from falling in your eyes.

✔ Wash any coating off your skin as soon as you can, and scrub up carefully after each session.

✔ Immediately clean paint off an animal's skin or fur—it can do serious harm, especially if the animal tries to lick it off. Wash away latex paint with plain water. Remove alkyd paint with a cloth soaked in mineral oil or cooking oil. Never use turpentine or any other powerful paint solvent: it will burn the animal's skin and will be doubly dangerous if the animal licks it off.

✔ Dispose of all paint, solvents, and other toxic chemicals in an approved manner. Call your local sanitation department or environmental protection office for advice.

The two major tools for any painting job are the roller and the brush. Rollers are by far the easier to use. They require none of the special handling necessary with brushes and can paint a wall or ceiling twice as fast as a brush can. On the other hand, brushes are more versatile, and most jobs need at least some brushwork to paint areas unreachable with a roller.

Choosing a Brush or Roller:
While a single roller may suffice for an entire job *(page 31)*, you will need more than one brush. Consult the guide on page 13 to see the different kinds of brushes.

You must also match the applicator to the paint. Natural bristles and fibers lose resiliency as they absorb water from latex paint, so use synthetics with latex-base coverings. For alkyd-base paints, either a natural or a synthetic material is fine.

Preparing the Paint:
Pigments sink rapidly to the bottom of a can of paint, the solvent rising to the top. So unless the paint has just been machine-agitated at the dealer's, mix it thoroughly before using *(page 32)*. Before doing so, however, check the paint to see if a skin has formed across the top. If so, use the procedure on page 32 to remove it. Never attempt to stir a skin back into the rest of the paint; the skin is insoluble, and stirring will only break it into tiny bits that show up on a newly painted surface.

Do not paint out of the original container. Instead, pour the paint into a pail, and keep the original can closed, so that the paint is less likely to dry out, get dirty, or spill. The tips on page 33 show how to keep paint clean and minimize drips and spills when pouring paint and moving it around as you work.

Using a Brush:
For the neatest results and to stave off fatigue, hold the brush correctly. The long, thin handle of a sash brush, for example, is most effectively grasped with the fingers, much as you would hold a pencil. The thick "beaver-tail" handles of wider brushes, however, are best held with the whole hand, as you would hold a tennis racket. Whatever the handle style, periodically switch hands or grips to keep your hands from getting tired.

In addition to the basic up-and-down brush stroke *(page 34)*, there are two important techniques. The first is "cutting in," or painting a strip in corners between two surfaces of matching colors *(page 35)*. At wall and ceiling edges where two colors meet, or on the narrow dividers between windowpanes, a technique called beading allows you to paint a sharp edge *(page 35)*.

 TOOLS

Paintbrushes
Roller cover
Roller frame
Extension handle
Roller with drop
  shield
Pail

Paint stirrer
Electric drill with
  mixer blade
Hammer
Paint shield
Corner roller
Paint pad
Roller pan with
  grating

 MATERIALS

Paint
Cheesecloth
Wire screening
Paper plate
Finishing nail
Aluminum foil

SAFETY TIPS

To minimize inhalation of paint fumes, always work in a well-ventilated area. When using alkyd-base paints and solvents, protect your hands with latex gloves.

BRURSHES AND ROLLERS

A design for efficient painting.
Whether natural or synthetic, the bristles of a typical paintbrush are frayed at the working end to hold as much paint as possible *(inset)*. At the other end, they are embedded in hard plastic, which is anchored to the brush handle by a metal band called a ferrule. Inside the ferrule, a spacer spreads the bristles at the base to create a thick, springy brush edge.

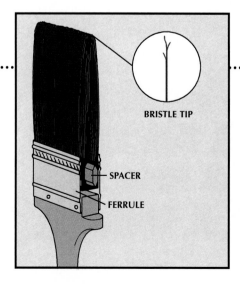

BRISTLE TIP

SPACER

FERRULE

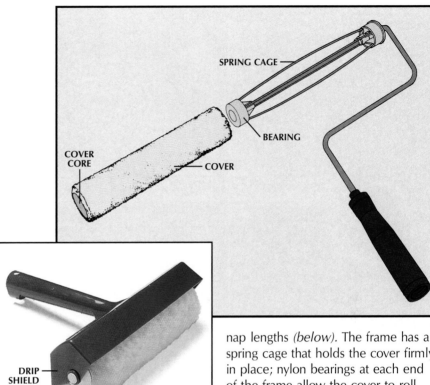

Anatomy of a roller.
Rollers consist of a cover and a frame, usually sold separately. Made of lamb's wool or synthetic fibers, the cover winds around a central core of plastic or cardboard and comes in a variety of nap lengths *(below)*. The frame has a spring cage that holds the cover firmly in place; nylon bearings at each end of the frame allow the cover to roll smoothly. To reach ceilings and high walls without standing on a ladder, screw an extension pole into the handle's threaded end.

For jobs where dripping paint may be a problem—such as when painting ceilings—purchase a roller frame with a built-in drip shield *(inset)*.

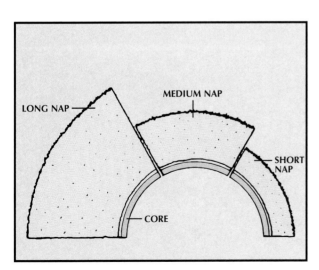

Choosing a nap.
Roller covers are available in three kinds of nap: short, medium, and long. Short nap, about $\frac{1}{4}$ inch deep, holds less paint than the others but leaves a thin, smooth coating that is ideal for glossy paint. All-purpose medium nap, between $\frac{1}{2}$ and $\frac{3}{4}$ inches deep, holds any type of paint well and produces a softly stippled effect. Long nap, from 1 to $1\frac{1}{4}$ inches deep, is good for working a thick coat of paint into textured or porous surfaces and leaves behind deep stipples in the paint.

Roller covers need no special preparation unless you are using glossy paint and a new, short-nap roller. In that case, prime the roller by sloshing it in soapy water to remove loose strands of material. Rinse the cover thoroughly and dry it completely before you begin.

PREPARING THE PAINT

Manual mixing.
◆ Pour the top third of the paint—the thinnest portion—into a pail.
◆ Stir the remaining paint to a uniform consistency with a wooden or plastic paddle.
◆ Gradually return the thinner paint to the can, stirring continuously until the paint is thoroughly mixed *(left)*.
◆ Pour the mixed paint from can to pail and back several times for a final, thorough blending.

TRICKS OF THE TRADE

A Better Stirring Stick

To make a wooden or plastic paint stirrer more effective, drill a few $\frac{1}{4}$- or $\frac{3}{8}$-inch holes along its length. As you stir the paint, the holes generate extra turbulence—resulting in quicker mixing.

Power mixing.
While faster than manual mixing, this technique requires more care, since you must keep the mixer's spinning metal blades from damaging the can's rustproof coating.
◆ Secure a two-bladed mixer to the chuck of a variable-speed drill and adjust the drill's trigger stop for a low speed.
◆ With the drill off, lower the mixer into the can until it touches bottom. Then raise it a few inches, keeping both blades submerged.
◆ Turn on the drill, and move the mixer around the can for a minute or two *(right)*. To avoid splatters, turn off the drill before withdrawing the mixer.

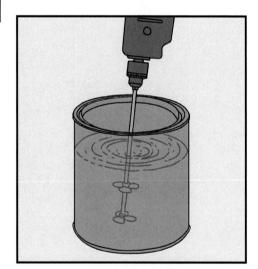

PAINT FILTERS AND DRIP CONTROL

Removing paint skin.
◆ Drape cheesecloth over a bucket, and secure the cloth to the rim with string or a rubber band.
◆ Gently separate the skin from the side of the paint can with a paddle.
◆ Pour the paint through the filter *(right),* then discard the cloth and paint debris.
◆ Mix the remaining paint as described above; it is not affected by the loss of the material in the skin.

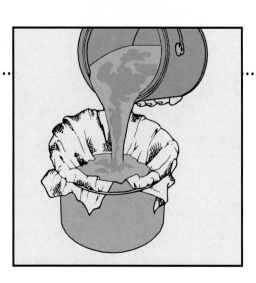

Keeping the paint clean.

This method is simpler than trying to fish out a brush bristle or other contaminant that falls into the paint.
◆ Cut a piece of window screening to the size of the paint-pail opening.
◆ Drop the screen onto the surface. The screen will sink, taking any debris to the bottom and trapping it there.

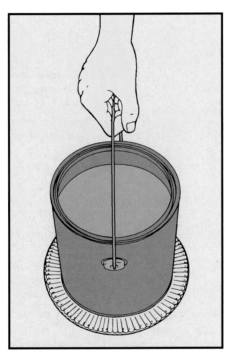

Drip-proofing the can.

A plastic-coated paper plate makes a simple drip guard. To ensure that the guard is always in place, secure the plate to the bottom of the can with loops of masking tape.

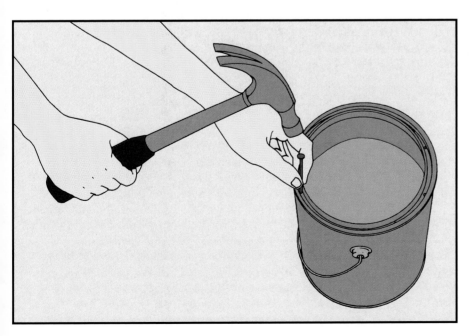

Preventing an overflow.

To keep the U-shaped rim of a paint can from filling with paint and overflowing, punch several nail holes around its circumference. Paint caught in the rim will then drain into the can, which can still be sealed for storage because the lid covers the holes. Keep the nail handy to reopen any holes that clog up with paint. Do not use this trick with cans smaller than a gallon; it may deform the rim, preventing the lid from making a tight seal.

BRUSHWORK BASICS

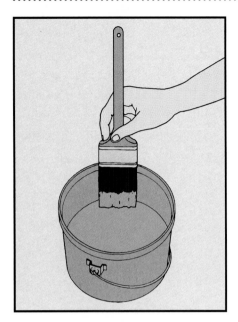

Loading the brush.
This technique helps prevent overloading and reduces the likelihood that paint will run under the ferrule, where dried paint can ruin the brush.

◆ Dip the bristles into the paint no more than halfway.

◆ Tap the ferrule gently against the rim of the pail to remove excess paint. Do not wipe the brush across the pail rim; doing so removes too much paint.

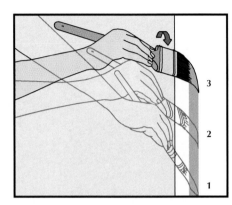

A feathered brush stroke.
Make the length of each stroke about double the length of the bristles. Wherever possible, end the stroke in the wet paint of a previously painted section.

◆ Start the brush stroke with the flat side of the brush angled low to the surface (1).

◆ As you move the brush, in-crease the angle gradually (2).

◆ End the stroke by drawing the brush up and off the surface with a slight twist (3); the brush should leave a thin, feathered edge of paint.

◆ If one stroke covers the surface satisfactorily, move on to an adjacent area. Otherwise, repaint the area with a second stroke.

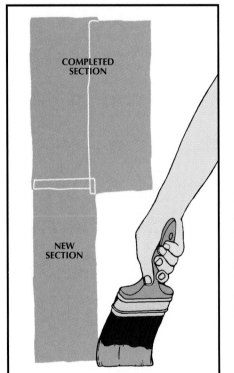

COMPLETED SECTION

NEW SECTION

Painting in sections.
Cover a large surface in sections, each about two brush widths across and two bristle lengths long. With slow-drying paints, you can experiment with paint-ing larger sections.

◆ Paint the first section, us-ing up-and-down strokes combined with the feather-ing technique shown above.

◆ Then move to an adjacent section, working toward and into the completed area of wet paint (left).

PAINT SHIELD

Guarding as you go.
A metal or plastic paint shield, available where paint is sold, protects surfaces you do not want painted.

◆ Hold the edge of the shield against the surface you want to protect. If there is a gap at the boundary, such as often occurs be-tween walls and baseboards

or walls and carpets, gently push the shield into it.

◆ While holding the paint shield in place with one hand, paint along the length of the shield with the other hand (left).

◆ Remove the shield and wipe it clean. Then reposi-tion the shield and paint the next section.

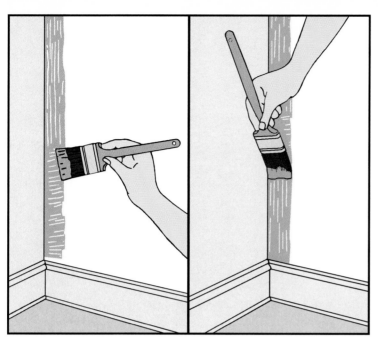

Cutting in.

◆ Make four or five 2-inch-long overlapping brush strokes perpendicular to the edge of the wall or ceiling *(far left)*. (At the bottom of the wall, make the last stroke about $\frac{1}{2}$ inch above the baseboard.)

◆ Smooth over the brush strokes with one long stroke. Wherever possible, end the stroke in an area of wet paint *(near left)* and use it to cover the small gap above a baseboard.

◆ Repeat this procedure along the edge of the adjacent wall or ceiling.

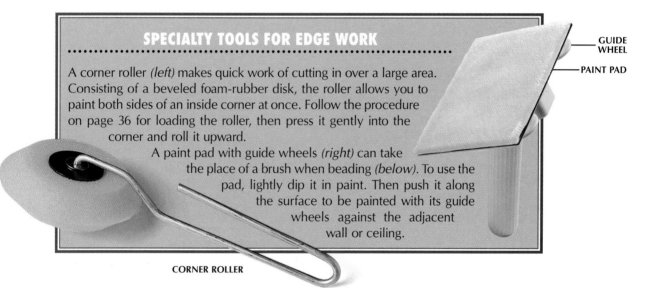

SPECIALTY TOOLS FOR EDGE WORK

A corner roller *(left)* makes quick work of cutting in over a large area. Consisting of a beveled foam-rubber disk, the roller allows you to paint both sides of an inside corner at once. Follow the procedure on page 36 for loading the roller, then press it gently into the corner and roll it upward.

A paint pad with guide wheels *(right)* can take the place of a brush when beading *(below)*. To use the pad, lightly dip it in paint. Then push it along the surface to be painted with its guide wheels against the adjacent wall or ceiling.

GUIDE WHEEL

PAINT PAD

CORNER ROLLER

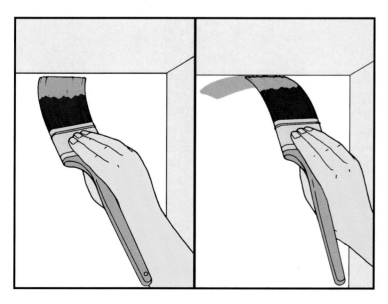

Beading.

This procedure works best with a stiff-bristled trim brush.

◆ Grasp the brush as shown here.

◆ Press the bristle tips against the surface near the edge, forcing a thin line of paint, called a bead, to emerge at the bristle tips *(far left)*.

◆ Then, in one smooth, steady motion, draw the bristle tips along a line about $\frac{1}{16}$ inch from the edge of the surface you are painting *(near left)*. Doing so forces the paint bead just to the edge of the surface.

LOADING A ROLLER

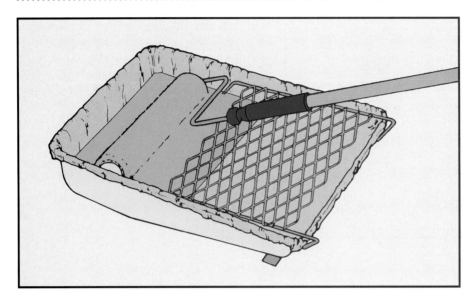

Distributing the paint evenly.
◆ Line a roller pan with aluminum foil to facilitate cleanup, then fill the well halfway with paint.
◆ Dip the roller in the paint, then roll it down the sloped grating, stopping short of the well. Repeat this two or three times.
◆ Dip the roller into the paint once more and roll it on the grating until the nap has been evenly saturated.

AN INITIAL ZIGZAG

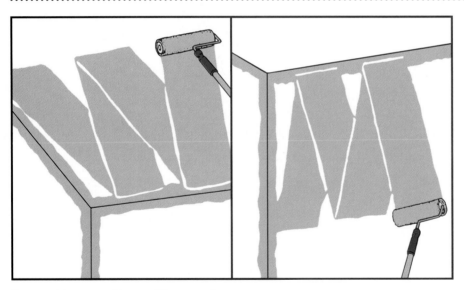

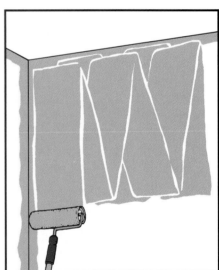

1. Starting a wall or ceiling section.
When painting with a roller, always make the first stroke away from you.
◆ To paint a ceiling, begin at a corner, about 3 feet away from one wall and overlapping the cut-in strip on the adjacent wall.
◆ Without lowering the roller from the ceiling, make three more strokes—alternately toward and away from you—to form a letter "W" about 3 feet square (*above, left*).

On a wall, push the roller upward on the first stroke and then complete an "M" pattern (*above, right*).

2. Completing the section.
Fill in the "W" or "M" pattern with crisscrossing strokes of the roller without lifting it from the surface. Use even pressure to avoid bubbles and blotches, and stop when the entire section is evenly covered with paint.

Reload the roller with paint, then repeat the preceding two-step sequence in the next section.

SPECIAL EFFECTS WITH PAINT

With a little extra effort and some simple tools, you can give an ordinary painted wall an eye-catching patterned finish. Stippling, ragging, sponging, and streaking, all shown below, are among the most popular methods.

A major appeal of these special finishes is that they draw the eye away from small imperfections in a wall or a ceiling. The thick paint that is used in stippling does even more—it can completely cover minor cracks and bumps.

The paint commonly used for these effects is available at most home-supply stores. Stippling requires a creamy, stucco-like covering known as textured paint, available in alkyd- and latex-base varieties. Sponging works with any type of paint, but a special glossy finish called a glaze is best for ragging and streaking.

Stippling

Since textured paint sets quickly, work in 3- by 3-foot sections. Begin by covering the first section with a $\frac{1}{16}$-inch-thick coat of paint, using a trowel, brush, or wide sponge-rubber applicator. Then pat the flat side of the tool against the wet paint. This raises peaks of paint on the surface, producing a deeply stippled effect.

Ragging

Apply a base color of alkyd semigloss paint to the wall. After the base coat dries completely, dip a clean, dry, crumpled rag into a glaze of the second color and dab it against the wall. Alternatively, you can roll a coat of glaze onto the base coat and dab it with a clean rag to reveal the underlying color.

Sponging

Cover the wall with the base coat, and allow it to dry completely. Then, lightly dip a sponge into the second color and dab it against the surface. The greater the pressure you apply with the sponge, the stronger the second color appears on the wall.

If you wish, you may sponge a second and a third color onto the base coat of paint, using a fresh sponge for each.

Streaking

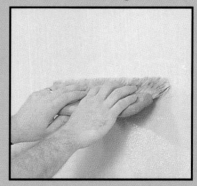

Also called stria, this technique gives the wall a gently striped effect that resembles wallpaper. After applying the glaze, drag a wide wallpapering brush vertically down the wall. If you need help keeping the brush straight, hang a plumb bob from the ceiling to serve as a guide.

To minimize drips and smears, work systematically from the top to the bottom of a room: Paint the ceiling first, then the walls, then windows, doors, and other woodwork, and finally the baseboards.

Ceiling and Walls: Plan on painting the entire ceiling and each wall without stopping. A roller attached to a 4- or 5-foot extension pole is ideal for reaching a ceiling. On a textured surface, be sure to use a roller with a long nap *(page 31)*.

On walls, some people prefer to paint in vertical portions from top to bottom. However, if you are using a roller on an extension pole to reach the top of the wall, you may find it easier to work horizontally, to avoid attaching the roller to—and removing it from—the pole more than once.

Windows and Doors: Painting double-hung windows in the sequence that is shown on the opposite page will solve the tricky problem of your having to move the sashes to paint surfaces that are obstructed by the lower sash. Paint the horizontal parts of the frame with back-and-forth strokes of the brush and the vertical parts with up-and-down strokes.

With doors, follow the techniques that are described on page 40 to achieve best results.

CEILINGS AND WALLS

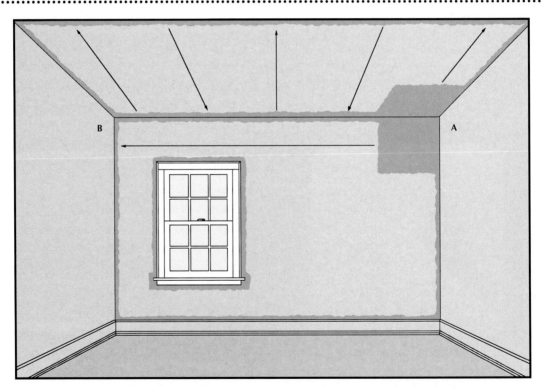

A basic pattern.
Paint a 2-inch-wide strip around the edges of the ceiling using the cutting-in technique described on page 35. Start painting the ceiling at a corner (A or B), then work back and forth across the short dimension of the ceiling in 3-foot-square sections, as indicated by the arrows. To prevent lap marks caused when wet paint is laid over dry, blend the paint at the edges of adjacent sections before the paint on either dries. After coating the entire ceiling, check your work for missed or thin spots, and revisit them with a roller lightly loaded with paint.

Before painting a wall, cut in not only along the edges, but also around the entire frame of any door or window and along baseboards. Apply paint across the wall in tiers, beginning at corner A or B and alternating direction as with the ceiling. Check your work for missed spots.

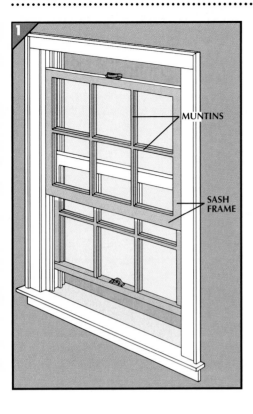

1. Start on the sashes.

◆ Raise the inside sash and lower the outside sash, leaving each open about 6 inches.

◆ Paint the inner sash first, omitting the top edge. Begin with the muntins (horizontals then verticals), followed by the sash frame (horizontals then verticals). Bead the paint onto the wood (page 35), allowing a narrow strip—about $\frac{1}{16}$ inch wide—to flow onto the glass and form a seal between the two materials. This irregular edge of paint is straightened during final cleanup (page 43).

◆ On the outside sash, paint the same parts in the same order as far as they are exposed—but do not paint the bottom edge until you paint the house exterior.

2. Complete the sashes.

◆ Push up on the bottom of the outside sash and down on the unpainted top of the inside sash, positioning them about an inch from their closed positions.

◆ In the same order as in Step 1, paint the surfaces of the outside sash that were obstructed; also paint the top edge of the inside sash.

◆ Proceed to paint the wood framing of the window, starting with the top horizontal. Coat the two side pieces next and finish with the sill.

◆ Wait until all of the paint is thoroughly dry before proceeding to the jambs in Step 3; meanwhile, work on other windows or on doors (page 40).

3. Finish with the jambs.

◆ When the paint is dry to the touch, slide both sashes up and down a few times to make sure they do not stick. Then, push both sashes all the way down to expose the upper jambs (left).

◆ Paint the wooden parts of the upper jambs in the order shown by the letters A through C; metal parts are never painted. Avoid overloading the brush to prevent paint from running into the grooves of the lower jambs.

◆ Let the paint dry, then raise both sashes all the way and paint the lower halves of parts A through C.

◆ Wait for the paint to dry, then lubricate parts A and B of the jambs with paraffin or with silicone spray.

CASEMENT WINDOWS

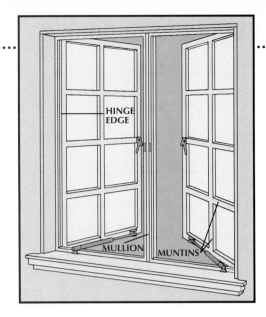

Windows that open outward.
Casement and awning windows may be made of aluminum, steel, or wood. An aluminum window does not need to be painted, but to protect the metal against dirt and pitting, consider coating it with a metal primer or with a transparent polyurethane varnish. Coat a steel casement with both a metal primer and paint, or with a paint especially suitable to metal, such as an epoxy or polyurethane paint. Treat a wood case-ment the way you would any other interior woodwork—unless the wood is clad in vinyl, which requires no paint.

Before painting, open the window. Working from inside outward and always doing horizontals first and then verticals, paint the parts in this order: muntins, sash frame, hinge edge, window frame and mullion, and sill. Leave the window open until all the paint dries.

DOORS, CABINETS, AND LOUVERS

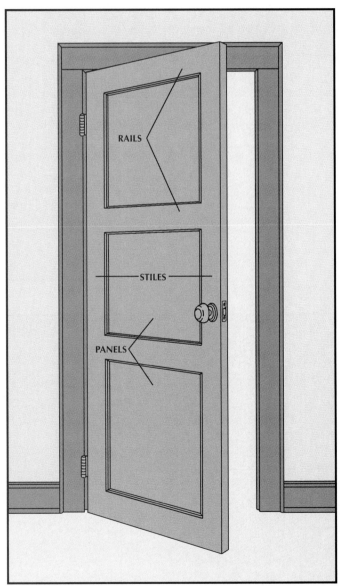

Hinged doors.
◆ Cover metal hinges, knobs, and latches with masking tape to protect them from paint spatters.
◆ Work from top to bottom when painting a door. On a panel door, shown here, paint the panels first, the horizontal rails next, and finally the vertical stiles. The top and bottom edges of a door need be painted only once in its lifetime, to seal the wood and prevent warping.
◆ Paint the latch edge only if the door opens into the room you are painting. The hinge edge of a door is painted the color of the room it faces when the door is open.

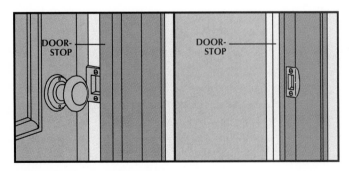

Doorframes and jambs.
◆ Paint the top of the doorframe, then the two sides, followed by the part of the jamb between the frame and the doorstop.
◆ Paint the doorstop as follows: If the door opens into the next room (*above, left*), paint the side of the doorstop that directly faces you and the broad side that faces into the door opening.
◆ If the door opens into the room you are painting, paint only the edge of the doorstop that the door closes against (*above, right*).

Painting a built-in cabinet.

◆ Remove all drawers; they will be painted separately.

◆ Work your way systematically from the inside of the cabinet to the outside, excluding the interior spaces where the drawers fit; they receive no paint *(right)*. Paint the walls first. Next, paint shelf bottoms, followed by the tops and edges. Do the insides of the doors before moving to the outside surfaces, painting from top to bottom.

Paint only the fronts of drawers *(inset)*. Do not coat the bottoms or exterior sides—paint there would prevent smooth operation. If you wish to paint the insides of drawers, do the sides first, then the bottoms.

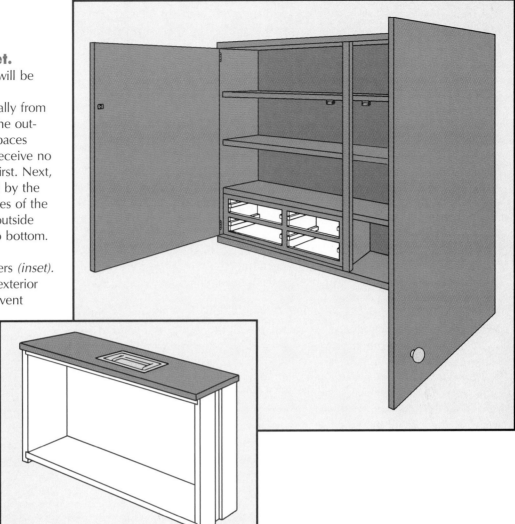

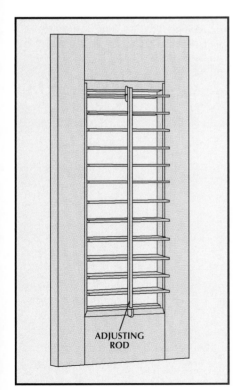

Solving the slat problem.

The narrow slats of a louvered shutter or door call for a $\frac{1}{2}$-inch brush and a slow-drying alkyd paint, so you have time to smooth drips on the slats.

◆ For an adjustable louver *(left)*, open the louver wide and set the slats to a horizontal position.

◆ Begin with the back of the panel so that you can smooth paint drips from the front.

◆ To avoid paint buildup where slats meet the frame, start painting at one end of a slat, flowing the paint toward the center in a long, smooth stroke. Repeat this technique at the opposite end of the slat.

◆ Cover as much of the slats as you can reach from the back side of the louver, opposite the adjusting rod.

◆ Turning the panel over, paint the inner edge of the adjusting rod, then wedge a matchstick or toothpick through one of its staples to keep the rod clear of the slats.

◆ Finish painting the slats one by one, smoothing out paint drips as you go.

◆ Next, paint the outer edges of the frame, horizontals first, then verticals. Paint the edges of the frame, and complete the job by painting the rest of the adjusting rod.

The slats of a stationary louver are set in a fixed, slanted position. Paint the backs first, from the ends toward the center. On the front, work the brush into the crevices between slats, then smooth out the paint with horizontal strokes.

41

Begin restoring a painted room to normal by pouring paint from buckets and trays back into the cans. Scrape as much paint as possible from the containers with a brush or roller. Clean the lip of the can and hammer the lid on tight.

Cleaning Your Equipment: Wipe buckets and roller pans clean using paper towels dampened with the appropriate solvent—water for latex- and vinyl-base paints, mineral spirits for alkyd-base products.

If you have been painting with water-base products, simply rinse brushes and rollers with warm running water. Use a paintbrush comb *(below)* to dislodge stubborn paint from brushes. To clean applicators of alkyd paint, fill containers such as coffee cans with enough solvent to cover a roller or the bristles of a brush. Agitate the applicator vigorously, replacing the solvent when it becomes saturated. Continue the process until the solvent is barely discolored, then run a paintbrush comb through the bristles.

Banishing Moisture: Dry brushes and rollers initially with a spin-drier *(opposite)*, then wash them in warm, soapy water. Rinse thoroughly, and use the spin-drier again.

Thoroughly dry brushes, hanging by the handle if possible; stand rollers on end.

Before putting away a brush, return it to its original package or fold it in heavy kraft paper *(opposite, top right)*. Hang it up or lay it flat for storage. Cover a roller with heavy kraft paper or place it in a perforated plastic bag to prevent it from becoming mildewed.

Final Touches: Cap thinners tight to prevent evaporation, and store them with leftover paint out of reach of children and well away from heat sources such as radiators and furnaces. Protect water-base paints from freezing.

Discard disposable dropcloths and paint-spattered newspapers. Check with local authorities as to disposal of used solvents and solvent-soaked paper towels. When the paint on window frames dries, scrape paint overflow from windowpanes as shown at the bottom of the opposite page.

⚠️ *Provide adequate ventilation to disperse toxic* **CAUTION** *fumes from solvents and thinners. Do not smoke near solvents and thinners or use them near an open flame.*

SAFETY TIPS

Wear gloves when working with alkyd-base paints and mineral spirits.

TOOLS

Paintbrush comb	Utility knife
Spin-drier	Ruler or putty knife
	Window scraper

Taking a Break

For interruptions lasting less than a day take the following precautions:

✔ If you will resume work within 15 minutes or so, simply rest your brush, unwrapped, on a support, never on its bristles. Leave a roller in the roller pan.

✔ For longer breaks, wrap wet brushes or rollers in plastic wrap or aluminum foil. Do not bind the bristles too tight.

✔ Cover paint that is left in a roller tray or pail tightly with plastic, or return the contents to the can and seal it. To avoid splatters, drape a cloth over the lid before tapping it in place.

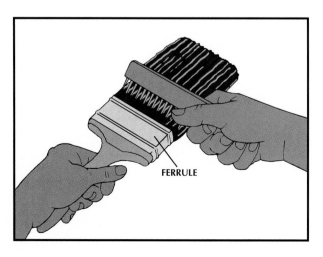

FERRULE

A comb for a brush.
◆ Push the sharp wire teeth of a paintbrush comb into the tightly packed bristles just below the ferrule, then pull the comb toward the tips of the bristles to loosen partially dried paint from the brush.
◆ At a later stage of the cleanup process, just before wrapping the paintbrush for storage, draw the comb through the bristles once more to straighten and untangle them. The brush is then ready for a future paint job.

SPRING
CLIPS

A spin-drier for brushes and rollers.

This cleanup aid spins excess solvent or water from paint applicators with a minimum of effort. To avoid spraying nearby objects, keep the brush or roller inside a paper bag, a bucket, or a garbage can with a plastic liner (not shown).

◆ Secure a brush in the drier by pushing the handle into the stiff spring clips *(left),* or slip a roller over them.

◆ Push the handle in and out of the tube to spin the brush or roller at high speed. Doing so throws paint-laden solvent or water from the applicator by centrifugal force.

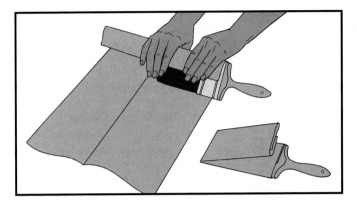

Wrapping a brush.

◆ Cut a rectangle of heavy kraft paper—a section of a grocery bag will do—about twice the combined lengths of the ferrule and bristles and about four times the width of the brush. Crease the paper down the center the long way.

◆ Place the brush on the paper as shown above and roll the brush into the paper.

◆ Fold the rolled-up paper at the crease. Secure it with a rubber band, making a wedge-shaped package that will preserve the bristles' taper.

A NEAT EDGE FOR WINDOWPANES

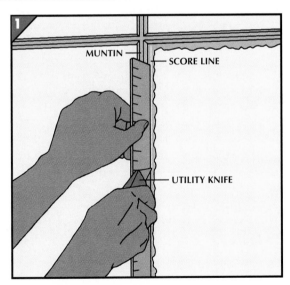

MUNTIN — SCORE LINE

UTILITY KNIFE

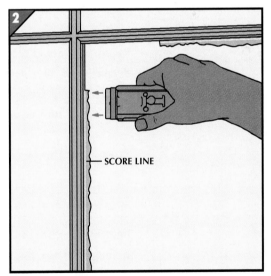

SCORE LINE

1. Scoring the paint.

With a utility knife or single-edged razor blade, score the paint on the glass, using a wide-blade putty knife or ruler as shown above to keep the score line at least $\frac{1}{16}$ inch from both sides of each muntin and from the sash or the casement frame.

2. Removing the paint.

Position a window scraper so that the blade is parallel to the score line, and carefully push the blade under the paint, stopping at the score. The paint will come off easily, leaving a neat, straight edge.

Painting Like a Pro—Outside

Coatings for the outside of a house are more protective than decorative, covering and sealing the exterior against the assaults of weather, airborne chemicals, and dirt. Exterior coatings are available for all the surfaces you may encounter—wood, masonry, metal—and include transparent and pigmented stains, which are applied in the same way as paint.

Painting clapboards →

Tool Kit for Exterior Work

Preparing and painting the exterior of your house will require, in addition to a ladder and a caulking gun *(pages 8-12)*, at least some of the tools shown on these pages. All of them are available at your local hardware or home-supply store. Heat guns *(opposite)* and wire brushes in an electric drill *(below)* can cause serious injury; consult the manufacturer's instructions for precautions specific to each tool. In general, however, wear eye protection when using a maul and cold chisel, using a wire brush in an electric drill, and when painting overhead. A respirator reduces the amount of dust inhaled when sanding.

> ⚠️ **CAUTION** *To reduce the chance of electric shock when working outdoors, plug power tools only into a receptacle protected by a ground-fault circuit interrupter (GFCI).*

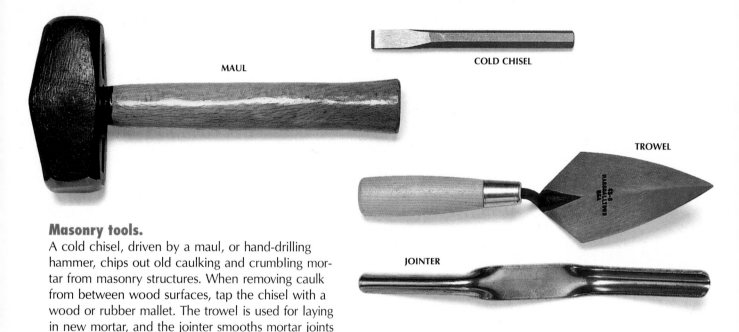

MAUL

COLD CHISEL

TROWEL

JOINTER

Masonry tools.
A cold chisel, driven by a maul, or hand-drilling hammer, chips out old caulking and crumbling mortar from masonry structures. When removing caulk from between wood surfaces, tap the chisel with a wood or rubber mallet. The trowel is used for laying in new mortar, and the jointer smooths mortar joints between bricks or concrete blocks.

DRILL WITH CUP BRUSH

Metal-restoration tools.
Wire brushes, either the hand-held variety or those intended for use with an electric drill, remove paint and rust from metal. Brushes for the drill—available in both cup and disk varieties—work faster with less effort but have a limited reach. To scrape areas inaccessible with the drill, use the hand brush.

DISK BRUSH

WIRE BRUSH

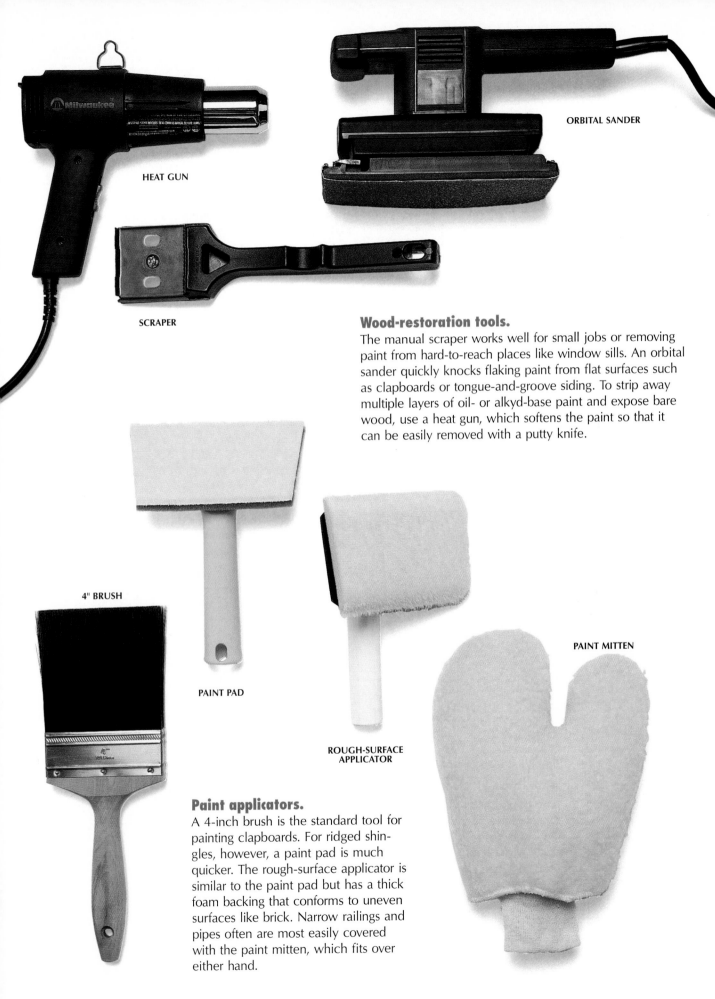

HEAT GUN

ORBITAL SANDER

SCRAPER

Wood-restoration tools.

The manual scraper works well for small jobs or removing paint from hard-to-reach places like window sills. An orbital sander quickly knocks flaking paint from flat surfaces such as clapboards or tongue-and-groove siding. To strip away multiple layers of oil- or alkyd-base paint and expose bare wood, use a heat gun, which softens the paint so that it can be easily removed with a putty knife.

4" BRUSH

PAINT PAD

ROUGH-SURFACE APPLICATOR

PAINT MITTEN

Paint applicators.

A 4-inch brush is the standard tool for painting clapboards. For ridged shingles, however, a paint pad is much quicker. The rough-surface applicator is similar to the paint pad but has a thick foam backing that conforms to uneven surfaces like brick. Narrow railings and pipes often are most easily covered with the paint mitten, which fits over either hand.

Diagnosing Paint Problems

Before you repaint the outside of your house, inspect the walls carefully. If you notice any stains, cracks, blistering, peeling, or other faults in the existing paint, consult these and the following pages to identify the source of the problem and how to fix it. Address these flaws before repainting; otherwise, the blemishes are likely to reappear, and over time they can result in damage to the house.

How Paint Problems Arise: Very rarely is the culprit the paint itself. More often it is a defect such as faulty construction that traps moisture in the walls, incomplete surface preparation on the last paint job, incompatible paints, or careless application. Though the examples shown here are more common on exteriors because of their exposure to weather, many of them can also occur on interiors.

Checking.

These short fractures along the grain of siding occur when paint loses its elasticity; as the surface expands and contracts with changes in the weather, the resulting stress causes the paint to break up. Remove the checked paint, as well as previous layers if there are more than two coats already on the surface. Prime the siding with a latex primer—it expands and contracts better than alkyd products—then repaint.

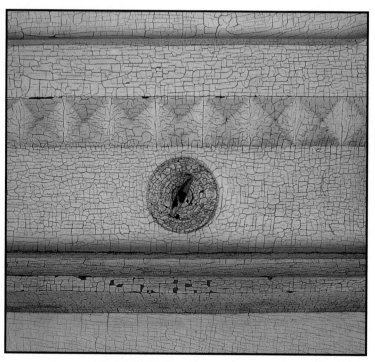

Alligatoring.

Scales like these result when the top coat of paint bonds poorly to the paint below it. The paints may not have been applied according to the manufacturer's instructions, or they may be incompatible with each other. Remove the cracked top layer and apply a new paint that is compatible with the surface.

Flaking.

As checking or alligatoring becomes severe, paint begins to flake off between cracks. In advanced cases, the large gaps left behind by flaked paint allow water easy access to the bare wood, which ultimately rots. Scrape off the flaked paint and prime the wood with a latex primer before repainting.

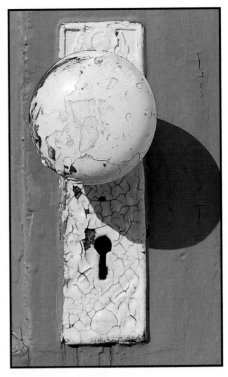

Flaking on metal.

If water penetrates the paint on a steel or iron fixture, the resulting rust can push the paint off the surface. Paint will also eventually flake if the fixture was not completely clean at the time of painting. Scrub the surface with a wire brush *(page 46)*, arrest any rust as described on page 59, then apply a fresh coat of paint.

Blistering.

More common with alkyd-base paints than latex paints, blisters pop up for two reasons. One is water vapor trapped under the paint; with no place to go, it pushes out against the paint. The other is painting a wall or roof whose surface temperature is above about 75°F. In such heat, a skin forms that traps solvent vapor to form bubbles. Scrape or sand off the blistered paint, then eliminate any source of moisture in the walls. Repaint only when the air temperature is between 50 and 75°F and the surface is not bathed in sunshine.

Peeling from wood.

This problem is often a consequence of blistering; as a blister grows, it tends to break loose from the wall. Peeling also occurs when paint is applied over dirt, grease, or loose paint. Scrape or sand off all loose paint and eliminate any sources of moisture in the wall. Repaint with latex primer and paint, since they are more permeable to water vapor than alkyds.

Chalk stains.

The brick wall above has been discolored by paint chalk that has washed down from the siding above it. Chalking paint helps keep the siding clean but should not be used where the chalk can streak areas below. The remedy for this situation is to wash the siding and repaint it with a nonchalking paint. Restore the brick by scrubbing it with detergent.

Rust stains.

Aluminum or stainless-steel nails and fixtures prevent this problem, which is caused by waterborne rust from iron or steel fixtures and nails that runs down the walls. Clean the rust from the metal, seal the metal with a rust-inhibiting coating, and scrub the stains from the walls.

Peeling from masonry.

Paint peels from masonry if it is applied to a heavily chalked or dirty surface. It also peels due to efflorescence, a process in which moisture drags salts within the masonry to the surface, where they crystallize and lift the paint from the wall. Strip the peeling paint, and check for sources of moisture; leaky pipes and gutters are often to blame. Follow the instructions on page 61 to wash away any salt deposits.

Mildew.

The dark discolorations on this window frame inside a house are the result of mildew fungus growing on the paint. Kill the mildew with a fungicide such as chlorine bleach *(page 53)*. And since alkyd paints contain organic compounds on which mildew feeds, use only latex paint on mildew-prone areas. As an extra precaution, choose a paint containing a mildewcide or add one to the paint yourself.

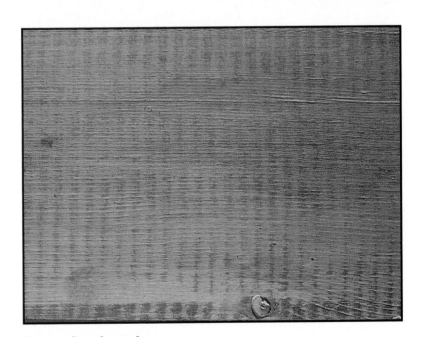

Dye and resin stains.

Redwood *(above),* along with woods like cypress and red cedar, contains natural dyes that can seep through a layer of paint. Use only alkyd primers and paints on such woods, as they cover dye stains more effectively than latex products.

The resin contained in wood knots often rises to the surface, where it can discolor the finish. Scrape the resin off the surface and seal the knots with shellac before applying new paint.

A high-pressure spray-cleaning device—which you can rent at many paint and hardware stores—reduces the labor of removing dirt, mildew, sea-spray salt, paint-chalk accumulations, or even peeling paint.

How a Spray Cleaner Works: A typical spray cleaner takes water from the supply system of the house or a barrel and pumps it out in a narrow jet at a pressure of 1,000 pounds per square inch or more, blasting off dirt and loose paint. The machine can also mix a variety of cleaning agents, stored in a reservoir on top of the pump housing, with the water for more efficient cleaning. Some models use only cold water, but others have a kerosene burner that heats the water for tough cleaning jobs.

 SAFETY TIPS

Wear rubber gloves at all times when spraying. Add a hat, long sleeves, long pants, and goggles when spraying a solution that contains liquid household detergent, bleach, or trisodium phosphate.

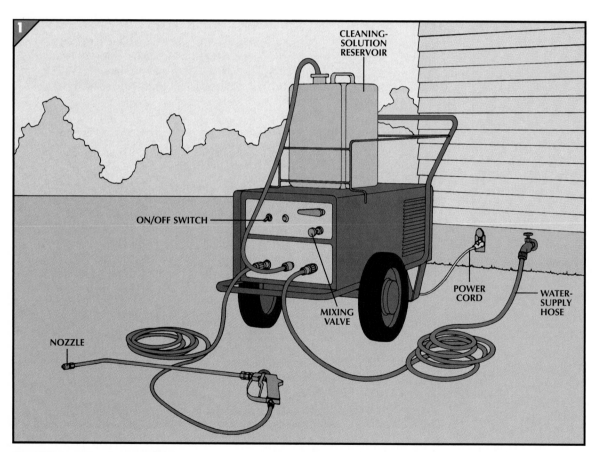

1. Making the connections.

◆ You must hook up three hoses to the spray cleaner before operating it: an ordinary $\frac{3}{4}$-inch garden hose to connect the spray cleaner with an outside faucet; a smaller hose, furnished with the unit, to couple the cleaning-solution container to the pump; and a third hose, also part of the equipment, to carry water and cleaning solution from the pump to the nozzle.

◆ Adjust the dilution of cleaner in the jet spray with a valve on the unit. Because powder granules may damage pump seals, use only heavy-duty liquid detergents for routine cleaning, or full-strength liquid chlorine bleach to remove mildew.

◆ Plug the unit into a receptacle that accepts a three-pronged plug and is protected by a ground-fault circuit interrupter. Heavy-duty extension cords equipped with this device are available for use with unprotected circuits.

2. Applying the cleaner.

◆ Fill the cleaning-solution reservoir and open the mixing valve to add cleaning solution to the water supply. For very grimy walls, turn on the heater, if your unit has one.

◆ Hold the nozzle 1 to 2 feet from the wall *(left)* and aim the stream parallel to the ground or slightly downward to avoid forcing water behind siding. Squeeze the trigger to spray, and beginning at the top of a section, sweep back and forth in 6- to 8-foot strokes. Continue working downward for about 10 minutes so the solution can loosen dirt and stains.

3. Rinsing off.

◆ Turn off the mixing valve in order to prevent cleaning agent from entering the rinse water.

◆ Start at the top of a section and hold the nozzle about 6 inches away from the surface and at a 45-degree angle in the direction you are moving. This allows the full force of the jet to shear off any loose paint chips.

◆ Spray across the section, from one side to the other. At the end of each sweep, reverse the direction of the 45-degree angle.

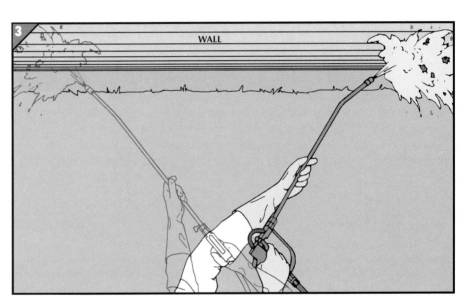

WALL

DOING AWAY WITH MILDEW

Mildew is a fungus that thrives on damp, shaded walls. Since it prevents new paint from adhering, you must remove it completely before painting. Scrubbing alone, however, is not sufficient to prevent regrowth; the spores embedded in the surface must be killed.

First, test stains that look as though they might have been caused by mildew. Apply full-strength liquid chlorine laundry bleach to the area with a rag. If the discoloration disappears in a few moments, it is caused by mildew. To remove it, make a cleaning solution of 1 to 2 quarts of bleach to 1 gallon of warm water. You can also make the solution with $\frac{1}{2}$ cup of an alkali detergent, such as trisodium phosphate (TSP)—if it is available in your community—dissolved in 2 gallons of water.

Remove any loose paint, then, for small patches, vigorously scrub the solution into the siding with a stiff-bristled brush. Tackle larger areas by spraying the solution from a high-pressure cleaner—preferably one that heats the water to 190°F. When the mildew is gone, flush the surface with water and let it dry before painting. Ask for paint containing a mildew-inhibiting agent, whether you use an alkyd- or water-base product.

Preparing the Surface

After cleaning the exterior *(pages 52-53)*, set to work removing various stains and making repairs to damaged brick, siding, and trim. Replace split shingles, cracked caulk around windows and doors, and loose mortar in brick walls.

Eliminating Stains: Rust and other metallic discolorations repel most paints, so these blemishes must be removed and prevented from recurring. If the stains are caused by leaks, stop them at the source: Seal joints *(pages 56-57)*, fix broken downspouts and gutters, and repair damaged roofs.

Steel nails in clapboard or shingle siding are a common source of rust streaks. If screens or gutters are depositing metal stains, scrape the metal clean with a wire brush and then coat it with an appropriate paint *(pages 122-123)*. Clear acrylic varnish will seal copper screens and prevent stains from occurring.

Removing Unsound Paint: Paint in poor condition—examples of typical deterioration are illustrated on pages 48 through 51—that did not come off with power spraying *(pages 52-53)* must be removed by other means. Follow the safety precautions for lead paint and asbestos described on page 15.

There is no need to remove all the old paint. Where it still adheres well to the surface, sand the edges of the paint smooth to help the new coat of paint form a continuous film. Also, roughen the surface of glossy paint with sandpaper to provide "tooth" for the new coat.

Hand sanders and scrapers are good for removing small patches of damaged paint from clapboard siding *(opposite)*. Where flaking is widespread, consider using an orbital power sander to speed the work. Hold the sander flat against the clapboard and keep the tool moving to avoid oversanding.

Around window trim and moldings, whose contours can make them difficult to scrape with a tool, chemical paint removers offer an advantage *(page 17)*.

While you are working on bare wood surfaces, seal any knots and oozing sap pores with shellac *(page 18)*. Repair areas of rotted wood typically found on window sills and at the bottoms of door casings and support posts *(pages 58-59)*. Most products for this task consist of a liquid wood hardener that solidifies and seals the wood and a two-part epoxy paste that fills in the damaged area. After drying, the filler is sanded and painted.

Peeling paint on metal and masonry surfaces usually comes off easily with a wire brush, although stubborn cases may have to be sandblasted by a professional. Chemical paint removers usually work well on metals but seldom work satisfactorily on masonry.

 TOOLS

WOOD
Sanding block
Hammer
Nail set
Stiff-bristled nonmetallic brush
Paint scraper
Orbital sander
Heat gun
Flexible putty knife
Wood chisel
Hacksaw blade
Rasp

JOINTS
Cold chisel
Mallet
Caulking gun

METAL
Stiff-bristled wire brush
Electric drill with wire brush attachments

BRICK & CONCRETE
Cold chisel
Maul
Stiff-bristled brush
Mortar hawk
Trowel
Mortar jointer

 MATERIALS

WOOD
Sandpaper
Exterior-grade wood putty
Primer
Oxalic acid
Stainless-steel or aluminum nails
Wood hardener
Epoxy wood filler

JOINTS
Caulk

METAL
Rust-converting sealer

BRICK & CONCRETE
Mortar mix
Muriatic acid
Ammonia
Primer
Aerosol degreaser

 SAFETY TIPS

Heavy-duty rubber gloves and goggles are essential when you are working with corrosive agents such as oxalic acid. Work gloves protect your hands from hot flakes of paint when you are using a heat gun. Wear a dust mask when sanding old paint.

Eliminating rust stains.

Lightly rub a surface rust stain on clapboard or other smooth siding with sandpaper *(far left)*, then sand down to bright metal the rusty nailhead that caused the stain. Coat the broad head of a common nail with a rust-converting sealer *(page 59)*. Do the same for the head of a finishing nail, but first drive the nail $\frac{1}{8}$ inch below the surface with a hammer and nail set. When the sealer dries, fill the nail hole with an exterior-grade wood putty, let it dry, and then coat it as well as any bare wood nearby with primer *(near left)*.

If rust has worked its way deeply into the wood, as often happens with shingles, sanding alone would remove too much material. In such a case, try bleaching the stain with oxalic acid (available at paint stores) applied with a stiff-bristled nonmetallic brush. If the discoloration remains, scrape and seal the nailhead, then prime the shingle before painting it with the rest of the house.

REMOVING PAINT FROM CLAPBOARDS

Scraping paint.

A rigid blade makes this scraper an efficient tool for removing small areas of flaking paint from house siding. Look for a scraper that also accepts a triangular blade, for working in corners, and a curved blade, for scraping concave shapes often found on door and window casings. With any blade, experiment to find the minimum pressure needed to take the paint off without damaging the underlying wood.

Removing paint with heat.

Sanding is the only way to completely remove water-base paints from siding, but a heat gun is a faster alternative for oil- and alkyd-base paint. Set the temperature according to the manufacturer's recommendations, then hold the heat gun a few inches from the surface until the paint begins to bubble and wrinkle. Scrape away the softened paint with a flexible putty knife or scraper.

⚠ **CAUTION** *Never use a heat gun to remove paint that contains lead unless you wear a dust-and-fume respirator rated for that purpose. Additionally, keep the area where you are working free of paper, wood shavings, and solvent-soaked rags, which can be ignited by hot paint that falls to the ground.*

Goggles protect your eyes when you are chipping old caulk.

RESEALING JOINTS

1. Removing old caulk.

Sealing with long-lasting butyl caulk requires joints that are completely free of old caulk. Use a cold chisel and mallet to remove it *(right),* then dust with a rag or brush. With other types of caulk, however, you need only clean loose pieces of deteriorated caulk from joints with a screwdriver or knife.

The Right Caulk for the Job

The chart below lists the five types of caulk most often used outdoors. Water-base latex caulks are easier to clean up than the silicone and butyl varieties but may not last as long. Check carefully that the caulk you buy is compatible with the surfaces that straddle the joint you wish to seal.

Type	Cleanup	Recommended Surfaces	Pros and Cons
Latex	Water	Glass, wood, metal	Paintable. Easy to apply and clean up. Available in colors. Apply in temperatures above 40°F. Limited flexibility, becomes brittle. Lifetime: 2-10 years.
Acrylic latex	Water	Glass, brick, wood, metal	Paintable. Easy to apply and clean up. Apply in temperatures above 40°F. Greater flexibility than latex caulk. Lifetime: 2-10 years.
Acrylic latex with silicone	Water	Glass, brick, wood, metal, concrete	Paintable. Available in colors, including clear. Apply in temperatures above 40°F. Stands up to weathering better than acrylic latex caulk. Lifetime: 5-15 years.
Silicone	Mineral spirits	Glass, wood, metal, concrete	Not paintable. Application temperatures vary by manufacturer. Excellent weathering characteristics. Fills large gaps better than latex caulks but tends to be more expensive. Lifetime: 10-50 years.
Butyl	Mineral spirits	Brick, wood, metal, concrete	Paintable. Inexpensive. Application temperatures vary by manufacturer. Good weathering characteristics, long-lasting. Ideal for joints subject to extremes of expansion and contraction and exposed to all weather conditions, such as for gutters and downspouts. Hard to clean up, slow curing time. Lifetime: 2-10 years.

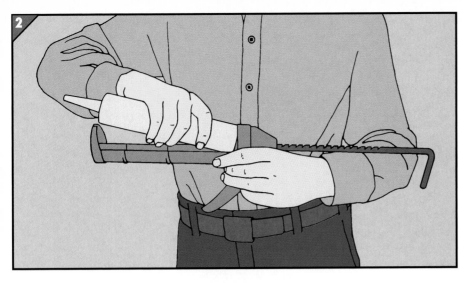

2. Loading a caulking gun.

◆ Turn the plunger rod until its teeth face up, then pull the rod back as far as it will go.

◆ Slip the cartridge into the gun, push the rod into the base of the cartridge, and turn the teeth facedown.

◆ Snip the plastic spout at a 45-degree angle to make an opening no more than $\frac{1}{4}$ inch wide.

◆ Silicone and butyl caulks are sealed. Insert a length of clothes-hanger wire into the spout to puncture the seal.

3. Applying caulk.

◆ Set the spout into the joint at an angle *(left)* and squeeze the trigger gently until the caulk begins to flow.

◆ Push the spout steadily forward along the joint while applying slow, consistent pressure to the trigger so the caulk fills the joint but does not overflow it.

◆ After filling the entire joint, run your finger or the bottom of a plastic spoon along the caulk to form it into a concave shape.

TRICKS OF THE TRADE

Caulking in Hard-to-Reach Spots

To reach joints that are all but inaccessible to a caulking gun—the top of a window frame on a house with a roof overhang, for example—jam a short length of vinyl tubing onto the spout. This flexible extension, affixed to the spout with duct tape if necessary, makes it possible to reach almost any joint.

Goggles protect your eyes from flying debris when you are splitting a shingle or stripping paint from metal with a wire brush or especially with a power drill.

REPLACING BROKEN SHINGLES

1. Removing a shingle.

Replace all broken or warped shingles before you repaint the house. Painting over bad shingles may disguise the damage but will also permit water to seep behind the good shingles and cause further deterioration.

◆ Split a shingle with a wood chisel along the grain, breaking it into narrow strips and slivers of wood.

◆ Wearing a glove to protect your hand, slip a hacksaw blade under the broken shingle and saw off the nails that hold it in place *(inset)*. Then pull out all the pieces of old shingle.

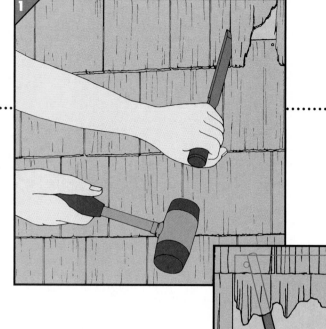

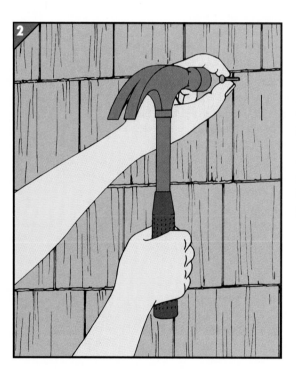

2. Installing a shingle.

◆ Slip the shingle under the course that is above and hold it in place.

◆ Drive two or three stainless-steel or aluminum nails through the new shingle just below the shingles that overlap it.

REPAIRING ROTTED WOOD

1. Removing damaged wood.

Rotted wood is gray and spongy. When probed with a sharp tool such as an awl, it crumbles, whereas sound wood cracks or splinters.

◆ With a scraper or chisel, carve out the rotted area until you reach undamaged wood *(right)*. Be sure to remove all the rot, even if you have to cut slightly into good wood.

◆ Using a brush or a squeeze bottle, apply a generous coat of wood hardener to all surfaces of the cavity and let it dry.

2. Filling the cavity.

◆ Mix two-part epoxy wood filler following the manufacturer's directions. These mixtures cure rapidly, so mix no more than you can apply in about 5 minutes.

◆ With a flexible putty knife, fill the cavity with the paste, being sure to compress it into all voids and cracks. Overfill the hole slightly and let the paste cure.

◆ Once it has dried, smooth the overfilled paste—first with a rasp, then with sandpaper—until the surface of the repair is smooth and flush with the surrounding wood.

◆ Prime the repair, then paint.

PREPARING METAL SURFACES

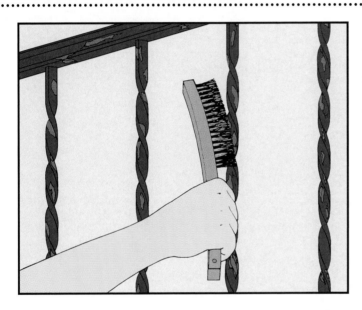

Preparing metal by hand.

◆ Remove any loose or peeling paint and corrosion from wrought iron and aluminum with a wire brush.

◆ Clean aluminum with a commercial solution that is specifically made for the purpose. Coat rusted wrought iron with a rust-converting sealer that chemically transforms the rust into a paintable surface.

Fast stripping with a power brush.

A wire brush attached to an electric drill shortens any metal cleaning task. A cup-shaped brush works best for broad surfaces like the face of a gutter (right); a wheel-shaped brush (inset) is better suited to corners and to smaller features such as gutter edges and wrought-iron railings. Always hold the drill so that debris from the brush flies away from you.

Work gloves and goggles offer protection when you are refurbishing brick. Switch to heavy-duty rubber gloves and add protective footgear and a respirator if you plan to work with acid solutions or concrete etchers.

RESTORING AND CLEANING BRICK

1. Digging out broken mortar.
◆ Chip out loose and crumbling mortar from between bricks with a cold chisel and maul. Take out enough mortar to expose bare brick on at least one side of every joint you repair; new mortar must have brick to adhere to. Chip deeply into the joint as well; it is better to take out some solid mortar than to leave broken pieces behind.
◆ Clean the dust from the joint with a brush.

HAWK

2. Laying in fresh mortar.
◆ Prepare a small batch of mortar from a packaged mix, adding water to make a mixture stiff enough not to run out of the joint.
◆ Brush water into the joint to wet the brick and prevent it from extracting moisture from the mortar. Do not use a hose; you may force water behind the bricks and damage the wall.
◆ Pile mortar on a hawk and press the mixture firmly into the joint with a trowel *(left)*. As an alternative, you can buy a mortar bag—which is similar to a cake-frosting bag—to squeeze mortar into the joints.

3. Shaping the joint.
◆ Use a mason's tool called a jointer, or striker, to force the still-wet mortar between the bricks and to give a smooth, even finish to the surface.
◆ After the mortar has dried—3 or 4 days—neutralize the alkalis in it, which can damage paint *(box, opposite).*

Efflorescence, a white, powdery crust often found on brick and concrete walls, is a major cause of peeling paint. It is caused when moisture in the masonry carries alkali compounds to the surface. As the water evaporates, the alkalis form crystals, causing paint to peel.

Efflorescence must be scrubbed away with a solution of 1 part muriatic acid to 10 parts water. If the deposits do not come off easily, make the solution stronger—1 part acid to 8 parts water.

After the masonry is clean, neutralize the acid by scrubbing with a solution of 1 part ammonia to 2 parts water. Then flush with a hose, working from the top of the wall downward.

Let the bricks and mortar dry for several days before painting. For best results on bare bricks, apply an undercoat of primer; otherwise the bricks may absorb paint unevenly, giving a mottled appearance.

⚠ **CAUTION** *To prevent dangerous splashes, always pour acid into water, never the reverse.*

TREATMENTS FOR CONCRETE

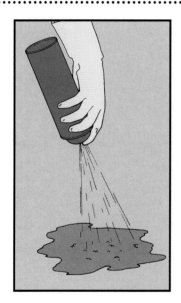

Using a degreaser.
Paint will not adhere to concrete surfaces that are slick with grease or oil. Spray a stain with an aerosol degreaser and let the solution stand for the time that is recommended by the manufacturer. Clean up and dispose of residue according to the manufacturer's recommendations; degreasers can harm grass or plants even if they are diluted by rinse water. Use a degreaser specifically labeled as safe for asphalt if you are working close to an asphalt surface. Let the surface dry completely before painting.

⚠ **CAUTION** *Vapors from these cleaners are flammable and toxic. Do not smoke while using them, and if you are working indoors, ventilate the area as thoroughly as possible.*

Etching concrete.
Before concrete is painted for the first time, etch it with a solution of 1 part muriatic acid to 5 parts water to neutralize the alkali in the concrete and roughen the surface to help the paint adhere. Scrub acid onto the concrete with a stiff-bristled brush. Once the solution stops bubbling on the concrete surface, mop it up and follow the manufacturer's recommendations for disposal.

⚠ **CAUTION** *To prevent dangerous splashes, always pour acid into water, never the reverse.*

Painting a House in Logical Order

Painting the exterior of a house calls for the same top-to-bottom strategy—and many of the same tools and techniques—as painting the interior. Careful planning is a necessity, due to the variety of exterior construction details.

Working High above the Ground: One way the exterior differs from the interior is in its scale. Painting the upper reaches of the exterior is more perilous than any indoor job. Extension ladders can help you do the sides of the house *(pages 8-11)*, but many houses have dormers that can be painted only from a sloping roof. If you use a ladder that reaches at least 3 feet above the edge, you can step safely from it onto the roof without standing on the top two rungs of the ladder or climbing over the eaves. While on the roof wear shoes with nonslip soles, use a ladder equipped with a ladder hook for foot- and handholds, and sit down as much as possible.

Applying the Paint: An exterior paint job has two major stages: coating the sides of the house and then the trim. Avoid painting in direct sunlight; begin on the shady side and do dormers first, leaving the overhang, trim, and windows for later. Continue down and coat the siding in horizontal strips, moving the ladder as needed.

Next, start on the trim. Again, begin with the dormers, then do the overhangs, gutters, and downspouts. Continue with the windows, shutters, and doors of the main part of the house. Paint door and window exteriors in the same way as their inside surfaces *(pages 38-41)*.

Finally, do the stair railings, stairs, and foundation. If stairs must be used before they dry, paint all the risers but only alternate treads, then do the rest after the first half has dried. Apply a coat of tough urethane varnish on wooden thresholds.

1	SIDING
2	TRIM
3	RAILINGS
4	PORCHES AND FOUNDATION

The sequence of painting.
This drawing shows the features that must be painted in a typical two-story house. The color key at left indicates the order, top to bottom in each case, in which elements of the house should be painted.

Special Methods for the Outside

Conventional brushes and rollers work fine on smooth exteriors like clapboard and siding. But there are some surfaces—such as cinder block, wood shingles, and narrow railings—that these ordinary applicators might not be able to handle. In such cases, the applicators and techniques shown on the following pages come in handy.

Spray-Painting: One option for outdoor work is to buy or rent an airless paint sprayer *(pages 66-67)*. The great advantage of this device is its speed—it can paint a house in just a fraction of the time it would take with brushes and rollers. Furthermore, sprayers can apply a thicker, more uniform coat of paint to the house than is possible with conventional applicators.

However, airless sprayers have their drawbacks. Because they operate under tremendous pressure, they can cause serious injury *(page 66)*. And because these sprayers produce a relatively coarse mist of paint, a chance breeze may blow paint in any direction. For that reason, some localities restrict the use of these paint sprayers and you must mask or move anything within a 10-foot radius of the sprayer that you do not want to be painted.

Using the Sprayer: Before starting work, read and understand the manufacturer's in-

structions for setting up, operating, and cleaning the sprayer. Also make sure the sprayer is equipped with the correct spray tip *(page 66)*. Thin liquids such as stains require a tip with a small opening; viscous fluids such as latex paint require a larger one. Generally, a tip that sprays a pattern about 8 inches high provides the best compromise between speed and ease of use.

To get the hang of spraying, first practice on a piece of cardboard or plywood. When you move to the house itself, start with an inconspicuous section, where mistakes can be corrected with a paintbrush.

 TOOLS

Paintbrushes
Pad applicator
Rough-surface
  applicator
Paint mitten
Paint sprayer

 SAFETY TIPS

Latex gloves protect your hands when you are working with alkyd-base paints and the solvents used to clean them from brushes and other applicators.

Painting clapboards with a brush.

Work in sections 3 feet wide and four or five clapboards high.
◆ Coat the bottom edge of each clapboard in a section *(left, top)*.
◆ Next, apply heavy dabs of paint along the face of one board *(left, middle)*.
◆ Then distribute the paint across the clapboard with horizontal brush strokes *(left, bottom)*.
◆ Finish the clapboard with a single horizontal stroke to minimize brush marks.
◆ Repeat the preceding steps for the next clapboard in the section.

Paint shingles in the same way you would clapboards, but cover their faces with vertical strokes, rather than horizontal ones, to follow the grain of the wood.

A pad applicator for shingles.

Consisting of a soft "rug" of short nylon bristles, the pad applicator works well on the uneven surfaces of shingles. As with clapboards, work in sections 3 feet long and four or five courses high.

◆ Apply the paint first to the shingle edges with the edge of the pad.

◆ Then paint each shingle face by pressing the entire pad firmly against the front of the shingle *(left)* and pulling downward with a single stroke.

A rough-surface applicator.

Similar to the pad used for shingles, the rough-surface applicator has a thick, spongy backing that conforms to the contours of brick and cinder block. Work the paint into the surface with a circular motion *(left)*, then smooth it out with straight finishing strokes.

A paint mitten.

Faster than any brush for coating narrow pipes and railings, this applicator is a bulky mitten covered with lamb's wool. Fit the mitten over either hand and dip it into a tray of paint. Lightly grip one end of the object to be painted with the mitten, then slide it toward the other end *(right)*. When finished, clean the mitten as you would a roller *(page 42)*.

POWER SPRAYERS

How the sprayer works.

At the heart of a paint sprayer is a pump run by a powerful electric motor. The pump draws in paint from a bucket through a pickup tube equipped with a coarse screen to trap foreign matter. The paint travels through a high-pressure hose, past a pressure regulator, and through a filter fine enough to capture particles that might clog the spray tip. An additional high-pressure hose carries the paint to the spray gun.

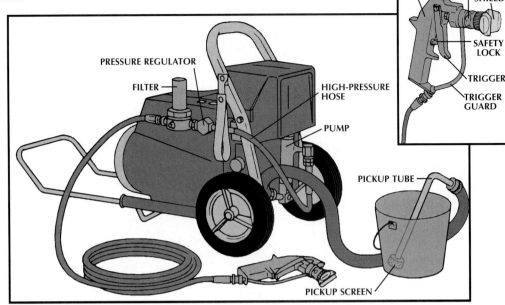

The gun itself *(inset)* is equipped with a trigger guard and a safety lock to prevent accidental discharge. A safety shield keeps fingers from getting too close to the spray tip.

Handling Sprayers with Care

Airless sprayers push paint through the spray tip at pressures up to 3,000 pounds per square inch, enough to inject paint through skin. If any part of your body is hit at short range by an emerging jet of paint or solvent, seek immediate medical attention. A hospital emergency room is the best place to go; your family doctor may not know how to treat this special kind of wound effectively. To prevent accidents, follow these safety rules:

✔ Always wear eye protection and a cartridge-type respirator when spraying.

✔ Make sure the sprayer you rent or buy has a trigger guard, a safety lock, and a safety shield around the spray tip *(above).* Keep the safety lock engaged when not actually spraying.

✔ Never point the gun at yourself or another person.

✔ Keep your fingers away from the spray tip. Never try to clear out the nozzle of a gun by pressing your finger against the spray tip while paint is being discharged.

✔ Do not disassemble the equipment for any reason without first turning it off, unplugging it, and then depressing the spray-gun trigger to release residual pressure in the hose.

✔ Keep children and pets away, and never leave the sprayer unattended.

A PORTABLE POWER SPRAYER

Instead of renting a commercial sprayer, you may wish to purchase a portable sprayer, available at home-supply stores. The smallest have 1-pint reservoirs that screw directly into the handle, and are suitable for painting items like fences and lawn furniture. Larger models *(below)* are intended for larger jobs—like an entire house.

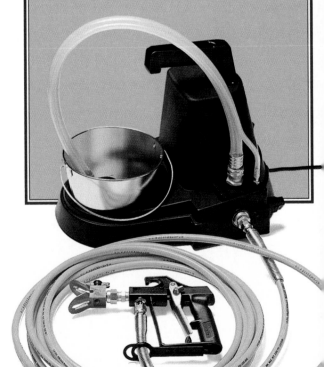

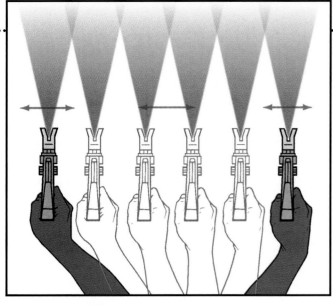

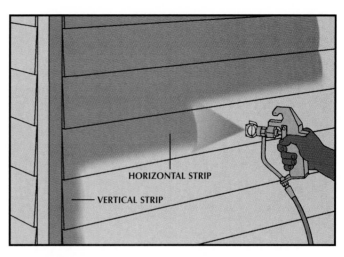

Gripping the spray gun.

The key to successful spray-painting is to hold the gun properly: perpendicular to the wall and 12 inches away. To maintain this constant angle and distance, crook your elbow slightly and bend your wrist *(above)*, so that you can move the gun in a line exactly parallel to the wall. For best results, do not spray a section wider than you can comfortably reach—about 36 inches for most people.

Covering a wall.

The best way to evenly coat a wall is to spray in a series of smooth, overlapping strips. Start the gun moving before depressing the trigger at the beginning of each stroke, and keep it moving after releasing the trigger at the end.

◆ First spray a vertical strip down the edge of the wall, releasing the trigger at the end of the stroke. This strip keeps you from spraying past the edge and wasting paint when applying horizontal strips.

◆ Then make a series of horizontal passes across the wall. Each pass should overlap the previous strip and the vertical strip by about an inch to compensate for the thin coating at the ends of the spray pattern.

DIAGNOSING SPRAYING PROBLEMS

The paint patterns illustrated at right are a tip-off that you are either holding or moving the spray gun incorrectly.

An hourglass-shaped pattern *(right, top)* results if you move the spray gun back and forth without bending your wrist to keep the sprayer the correct 12-inch distance from the wall. As the gun arcs past the wall, it first moves closer to the wall and then farther away, leaving a wide thin coat at the ends of the strip and a narrow thick coat at the center.

Tilting the gun while spraying causes a different kind of unevenness *(right, bottom)*. If the gun is pointed slightly downward, the resulting layer of paint will be denser at the top of the spray pattern than it is at the bottom. The reverse occurs when the gun is pointed upward.

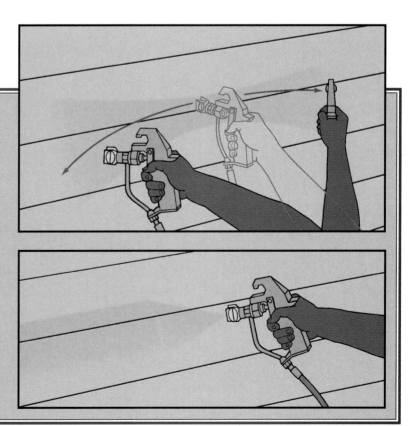

3 Wallpapering for Everyone

Wallpaper, an attractive alternative to paint, is easier to install than ever. New paper, vinyl, and fabric wall coverings, more durable than their predecessors, are often pretrimmed and prepasted. They are also tear- and crease-resistant, washable, and more easily removed. Take the time to plan ahead: An appropriate wall covering, adhesive, and choice of pattern will afford the most pleasing results.

Smoothing wallpaper at a baseboard →

Tool Kit for Paperhanging

The paperhanging tools shown here are grouped according to the various stages of preparing a room for a wall covering and hanging the paper.

Not every tool in this collection is necessary for every job. The water box, for example, is needed only for prepasted papers, and the artist's brush is used mostly for small repairs to damaged or peeling wallpaper. Tools like the trimming knife and the utility knife are interchangeable. Some do double duty; a utility knife and the seam roller, for example, are as helpful for minor repairs on previously hung paper as they are in hanging new paper.

All these tools are available at home-improvement and decorating stores; many are packaged as a complete wall-covering tool kit. If you are acquiring tools separately, buy only those you need for your project.

Scraping and repairing.
A wall scraper is the tool used to remove paper without wetting it or to break the surface for soaking. A wide, flexible putty knife helps peel a soaked covering away from a wall. You need a narrower, rigid putty knife if the walls must be repaired before the new covering is applied.

Measuring and marking.
A metal straightedge at least 36 inches long takes measurements and guides long cuts. A plumb bob helps you establish a precise vertical line. The chalk line marks a straight line on a wall; the string coats itself with powdered chalk stored in the case.

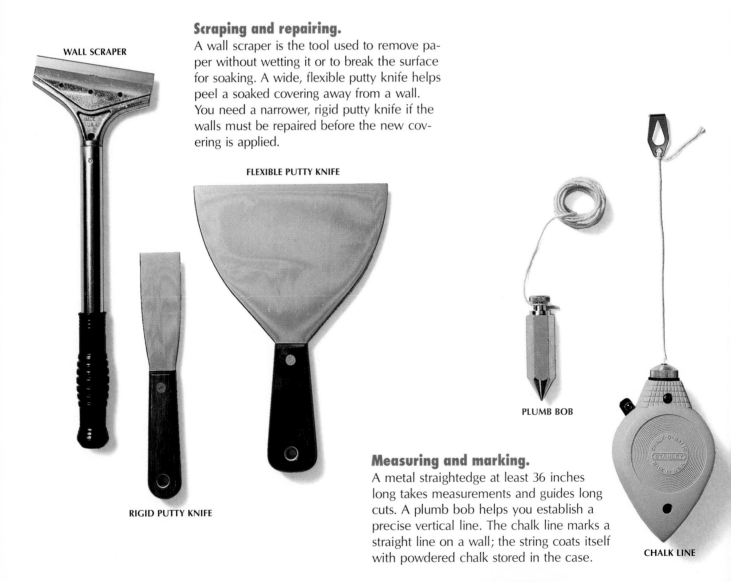

WALL SCRAPER

FLEXIBLE PUTTY KNIFE

RIGID PUTTY KNIFE

PLUMB BOB

CHALK LINE

METAL STRAIGHTEDGE

WATER BOX

ARTIST'S BRUSH

PASTE BUCKET

Pasting.

A paste bucket and brush are used to mix and apply adhesive. Water boxes come in several sizes; an extra-long one lets you soak two strips of prepasted paper at a time. The artist's brush is ideal for pasting small tears or peeling corners.

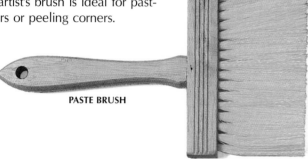

PASTE BRUSH

SEAM ROLLER

TRIMMING GUIDE

Cutting.

Wallpaper can be cut with scissors, a utility knife, or a trimming knife. This utility knife has a segmented blade; snap off the tip when it dulls. The trimming knife uses a single-edged razor blade.

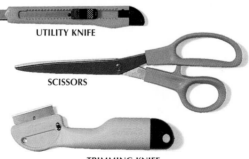

UTILITY KNIFE

SCISSORS

TRIMMING KNIFE

Edging and rolling.

The metal trimming guide creases paper against the wall at a ceiling or baseboard for cutting. A seam roller gives a final smoothing to edges.

SPONGE

SMOOTHING BRUSH

Smoothing and cleaning.

A smoothing brush fixes the paper firmly on the wall. The sponge is for wiping up stray adhesive. For prepasted papers, a sponge is recommended for smoothing instead of the brush.

Whatever type of surface you are papering over—wood, new wallboard or plaster, paint, a stripped wall, or existing paper—the wall must be properly prepared if the new paper is to adhere well.

Preparing a Painted Surface: Before papering over paint, wash the wall with a household cleaner to remove mildew, dirt, and grease, and rinse well. Lightly push a flexible putty knife along the walls to knock off any loose material and also to help you find popped nails or other imperfections in the wall. Repair damaged surfaces as described on pages 20 through 27, then coat the wall with an opaque all-purpose primer-sealer, which is compatible with all types of papers and adhesives.

Primer-sealer prevents paste from being absorbed into the wall and provides a surface for the new paper to glide onto easily. It binds chalking paint, eliminating the need to remove an old finish, and it roughens semigloss and satin paints for good paper adhesion.

Stripping Paper: Whenever possible, remove old paper; new coverings will always adhere better to a stripped wall. Vinyl or vinyl-coated coverings, which can be identified by their smooth, plastic textures, are called strippable papers because they are easily pulled from a wall. If a test pull at a top corner gets no results, you are probably dealing with a nonstrippable material or a strippable paper applied over unprimed wallboard. Try removing the paper by soaking or steaming *(pages 73-75)*.

If these methods fail—as may happen in a bathroom covered with a vinyl material stuck to the wall with waterproof adhesive—you can dry-scrape the wall *(opposite)*. Once you have stripped the paper, prepare the walls as you would a painted surface.

Papering over Paper: You may decide to apply new paper over an existing wall covering because the wall beneath is too fragile to withstand paper stripping, or because the time you save by leaving the old paper on the wall is more important than the long-term durability of the job.

Applying new wallpaper over old, however, is risky: the water in wallpaper paste can loosen old layers so they pull away from the wall. Make sure the old covering is firmly attached to the wall and as smooth as possible.

Never attempt to paper over more than three layers of paper, no matter how well they seem to be attached. The weight of the additional layer, plus wet wallpaper paste, can pull away the whole sheaf of papers.

Apply spackling compound to smooth the seams, and coat the old paper with opaque all-purpose primer-sealer. If you are applying new paper to vinyl, you must use a vinyl-to-vinyl adhesive, even if the new paper is prepasted.

Final Preparations: Before getting ready to apply new paper, refinish the trim and paint the ceiling if these are part of your redecorating plan. While it is simple to wipe wallpaper paste from woodwork, cleaning paint from new wallpaper is next to impossible.

TOOLS

Flexible putty knife (3" or 4")
Utility knife
Wall scraper
Sponges
Cheesecloth
Wallpaper steamer

MATERIALS

Water
Chemical stripping solution
Primer-sealer

SAFETY TIPS

When you are working with chemical stripping solutions, rubber gloves and goggles are essential. A dust mask prevents droplets of the solution from getting in your mouth and nose.

STRIPPING AND SCRAPING OLD PAPER

Removing strippable wall coverings.

◆ With a fingernail or a utility knife, lift a corner of the covering at the top of a section.

◆ Carefully peel the covering downward, pulling it flat against itself *(left)* to minimize ripping of the paper backing.

◆ Remove any backing that remains stuck to the wall, but leave the fuzzy residue to help the new wall covering adhere.

If the paper surface of wallboard peels off with the wall covering, it was applied without a primer-sealer. Soak the material to remove it *(below)*, or repaste the corner and apply the new wall covering over the old.

Dry-scraping paper.

Nonstrippable papers that cannot be soaked off because of waterproof adhesives must be removed from the wall using a wall scraper.

◆ Hold the blade of the scraper perpendicular to the wall and slit the paper horizontally. Apply gentle pressure to avoid damaging wallboard behind the paper.

◆ Slide the blade into a slit at an angle and loosen a section of paper at a time. Tear the loosened sections off with your fingers.

SOAKING PAPER TO REMOVE IT

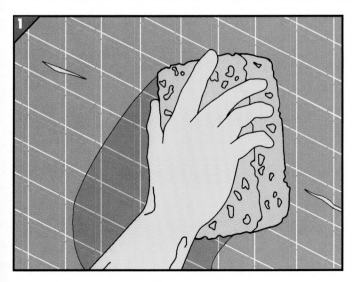

1. Wetting the paper.

A stripping solution of ethyl alcohol and other chemicals or a liquid containing enzymes that break down the organic materials in wallpaper paste works more quickly than plain water.

◆ Spray the paper with a small amount of water. If the water penetrates, there is no need to perforate the paper. Otherwise, you must puncture the paper so that stripping solution can get behind it. Use either the blade of the scraper *(above)* or the perforating tool shown on page 74.

◆ With a large sponge or a garden sprayer set for a fine stream, not a mist, wet all the walls with stripping solution.

◆ Wait 5 to 10 minutes—or the length of time recommended by the manufacturer—then wet the first wall again and proceed to Steps 2 and 3. (Always resoak a wall before beginning to strip paper.)

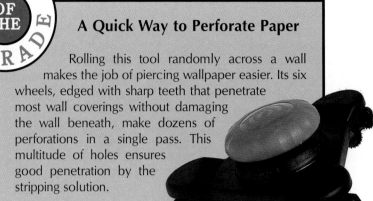

A Quick Way to Perforate Paper

Rolling this tool randomly across a wall makes the job of piercing wallpaper easier. Its six wheels, edged with sharp teeth that penetrate most wall coverings without damaging the wall beneath, make dozens of perforations in a single pass. This multitude of holes ensures good penetration by the stripping solution.

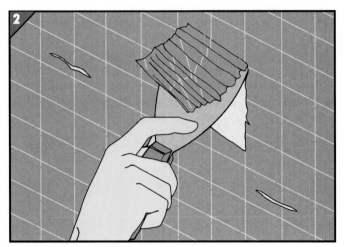

2. Loosening the paper.

Holding a putty knife at about a 30-degree angle, firmly push the wet paper up from one of the perforations in the paper. The paper should come up easily *(left)*. If it does not, resoak and try again. Where the stripping solution fails to soften the paste, you will have to use a steamer *(opposite)*.

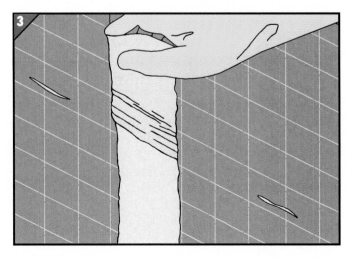

3. Stripping paper away.

◆ Grasp the loosened paper with your fingers and draw upward steadily and firmly *(left)*. To help prevent the paper from ripping, pull it parallel to the wall.
◆ After stripping off all the paper in the room, wash the walls with cheesecloth dipped in the stripping solution to remove any of the remaining scraps of wallpaper and paste.

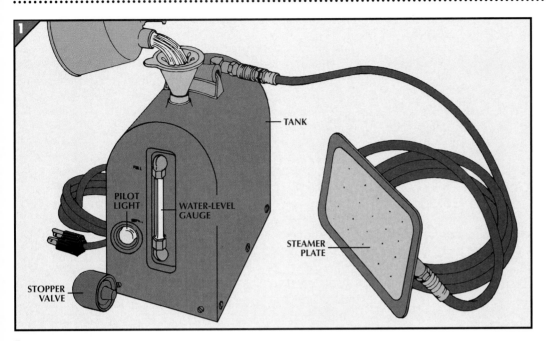

1. Starting the steamer.

When soaking fails, rent an electric steamer, available at most wallpaper dealers. Typically, the device consists of a boiler and a perforated plate that applies the steam to the wall covering.

◆ To fill the tank, unplug the cord and remove the stopper valve at the top.

◆ Set a funnel in the opening, and pour in boiling water until the water-level gauge indicates full.

◆ Plug in the steamer; a pilot light shows when the unit is on. The steamer is ready to use when vapor comes from the steamer plate.

2. Using the steamer plate.

◆ Hold the plate firmly against the wall without moving it.

◆ When the paper around the plate darkens with moisture or water droplets run down the wall, move the plate onto an ad-jacent area in the same strip of paper and repeat the steam-ing process.

◆ When you have steamed half a strip, proceed to Steps 2 and 3 on the preceding page to re-move the paper.

Wallpaper goes on the wall in consecutive strips, both clockwise and counterclockwise from the first one, with the pattern of each matching the previously completed section. Since the pattern unfolds from the starting point, the placement of the first strip affects the entire wallpapering job. Designs with narrow stripes and small random patterns match easily and can be begun conveniently alongside any door or window. But before you begin to hang a complex pattern, make sure you choose your starting point carefully.

Getting the Pattern Right: Complex patterns usually look best when the overall arrangement is symmetrical and the strips placed so the pattern draws a viewer's attention to a single part of the room—one wall, or the space above a fireplace, or the area surrounding one or more windows. When planning such an arrangement, try to avoid hanging strips whose width is less than

6 inches; they may be difficult to align and to affix.

Before putting up the first strip, inspect the wallpaper and note if the pattern is centered on the roll. If it is not, move the roll to the left or right to center the pattern on the wall rather than the roll.

Ensuring Alignment: When you hang the first strip and periodically thereafter, check to make sure that the paper is going on straight. Use a chalk line, metal straightedge, or carpenter's level to make vertical lines on the walls, and align the paper with them as you proceed *(page 79)*.

A Suitable Finish: Unless the room contains an interruption on one wall such as a floor-to-ceiling storage unit or a built-in corner cabinet, a mismatch will occur along one edge of the last strip. Plan ahead to locate the mismatch in an inconspicuous place *(page 78)*.

LOCATING THE FIRST STRIP

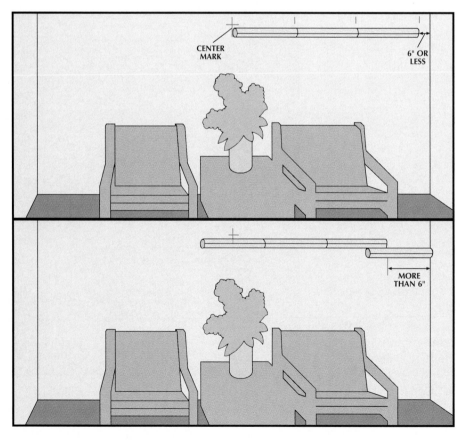

CENTER
MARK

6" OR
LESS

MORE
THAN 6"

To center on a wall.

◆ Locate and mark the center of the wall. Then, using a roll of wallpaper, measure the distance to the nearest corner: place one edge of the roll against the mark and move the roll toward the corner, one width at a time, until less than the width of one roll remains.

◆ If the remaining distance is 6 inches or less *(left, top)*, plan to center the first strip of paper over the mark *(left, bottom)*. If the remaining distance exceeds 6 inches, hang the first strip of paper where you started measuring—with the left edge of the strip against the pencil mark.

◆ To center the pattern above a fireplace, make the pencil mark above the center of the mantel and proceed as for a wall.

To center between two windows.

The width of the wall between the windows determines the placement of the first strip of wallpaper.

◆ With a pencil, mark a spot that is halfway between the windows and then center a roll of paper on that mark.

◆ If centering the roll on the mark results in narrow strips at each window edge *(above, left)*, you may prefer to hang the first strip alongside the center mark *(above, right)*.

To center above a window.

◆ Mark the center of the wall section above the window and measure as for walls *(opposite)*, moving the roll toward the window's right upper corner.

◆ If the last full roll of wallpaper extends 6 inches or less beyond the corner of the window *(above, left)*, plan to center the first strip on the mark *(above, right)*.

PLANNING THE LAST STRIP

To end at a floor-to-ceiling interruption.

If a wall you plan to paper contains a section of paneling, a fireplace, or a built-in cabinet or bookcase, as in the illustration at left, make this area the target of your final strip. After you choose the location of your first strip *(pages 76-77),* work from there both clockwise and counterclockwise, ending at the left and right sides of the interrupted area. In this way, there will be no mismatched strip anywhere.

To end in a partly hidden area.

An unobtrusive corner is best for ending in mid-pattern. In the room above, for example, the shallow corner where the fireplace meets the wall gets no direct light from the nearest window and is inconspicuous from most directions. Another option might be a corner of the room that is obscured by furniture.

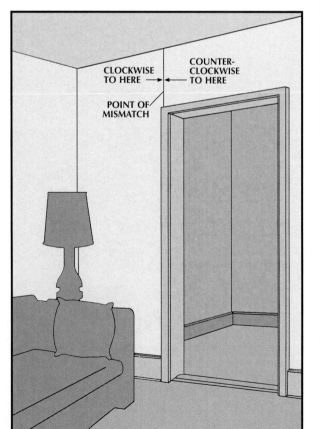

To end above a door.

The narrow strip of wall above a door is a likely place to finish papering. Join the last two strips above the side of the door that is closer to the room's nearest corner *(left).* If the door is centered on the wall, consider the location of windows and lamps and choose the side of the door that receives less light.

GETTING THE PATTERN STRAIGHT

No house has truly vertical walls. If you hang strips of wallpaper by following the planes of the walls, the paper will be uneven by the time you finish the job.

To avoid slanted strips, draw a true vertical line and align the first strip with it. Recheck the alignment frequently, particularly after turning a corner; doing so enables you to move the paper before the adhesive dries. Two simple tools for marking a vertical line on a wall, a chalk line and a metal straightedge, are illustrated here.

Before putting up chalked lines, test one with your wallpaper; the chalk may show through some translucent or light-colored papers. You can substitute a carpenter's level for the straightedge; read both upper and lower vials to make sure that the level is truly vertical. Then press the level firmly against the wall and draw a pencil line along its side.

CHALK LINE CASE

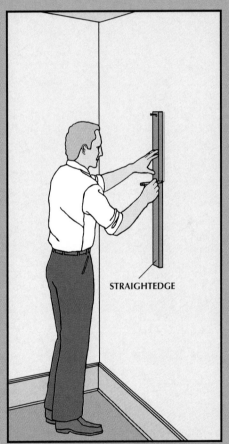

STRAIGHTEDGE

Chalk line.
◆ Tack the end of a chalk line high on the wall; when the case stops swinging, the string will be vertical.
◆ Without altering the position of the case, pull it slightly downward until the string is taut, press it firmly against the wall, and snap the string with the other hand (above).

Metal straightedge.
◆ Tack a metal straightedge loosely to the wall through the hole in one end.
◆ When the straightedge comes to rest, hold it firmly against the wall and draw a light pencil line along its edge (above).

A Mess-Free Pasting Method

Unless you use prepasted paper and a water box *(opposite, bottom)*, the choice of an adhesive and its correct application have much to do with the success of a wallpapering project. Purchase the one recommended by the wall-covering manufacturer; if no such instructions accompany the wallpaper, follow your dealer's advice.

Types of Adhesive: Whether organic or synthetic, adhesives are available in both liquid and dry form. Pour liquids directly into a bucket if you plan to apply with a paste brush, or into a roller tray for a paint roller. Dry adhesives must be mixed with water; directions on the package indicate how much. Approximately 30 minutes before use, pour the powder slowly into the water to minimize lumps. Mix thoroughly, making sure that you dissolve all lumps.

Applying the Paste: In order to spread adhesive evenly over the back of a strip of wallpaper, you'll need a table at least half as long as the strip. Neatness counts in pasting; avoid getting adhesive on the pattern side—or on the table where the next strip of wallpaper would come in contact with it. One way of achieving this is to spread several layers of kraft paper on the table, discarding the top layer after applying the paste to each strip. The method demonstrated here, however, eliminates waste by keeping the brush well away from the table surface during the entire operation.

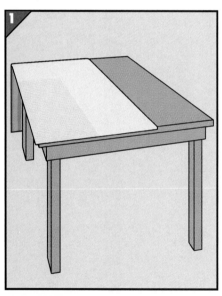

1. Pasting the lower left area.
◆ Measure and cut the wallpaper into strips *(page 82)*, then lay one strip on the table, pattern side down, so that the left and lower edges extend beyond the table a quarter inch or so.
◆ Apply paste to the lower left quarter, covering a little less than half the length of the strip.

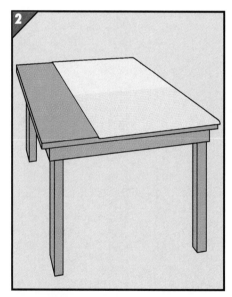

2. Pasting the lower right area.
◆ Shift the strip across the table, allowing the strip's right and lower edges to jut slightly beyond the tabletop.
◆ Paste the lower right quarter.

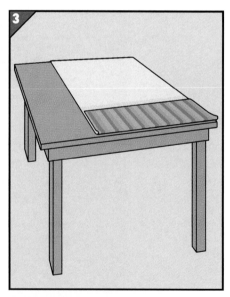

3. Making the lower fold.
Pull the strip toward you, and without creasing the paper, gently fold the pasted section onto itself, pattern side out. Make this fold somewhat shorter than the one you will make at the top *(Step 6)* so you can identify the top when you are ready to hang the strip.

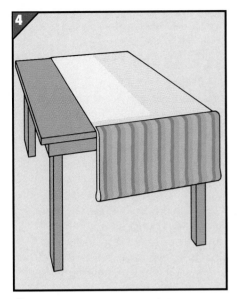

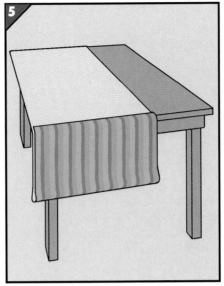

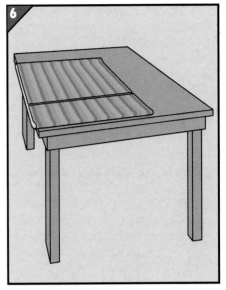

4. Pasting the upper right area.

◆ Slide the strip toward you until the upper edge of the paper barely overlaps the table. Let the folded section hang freely over the edge of the table, and make sure that the right edge of the paper still extends beyond the right edge of the table.

◆ Paste the upper right quarter of the wallpaper strip.

5. Pasting the upper left area.

◆ Shift the strip to the left across the table to position the strip's left and upper edges slightly beyond the edge of the table.

◆ Paste the upper left quarter.

6. Making the top fold.

◆ Fold the upper section onto itself as you did the lower section in Step 3, bringing the top edge just short of the bottom edge. Do not crease the fold.

◆ Set the pasted strip on a clean surface to cure for about 10 minutes; the strip will then be ready to hang *(pages 82-84)*. While you are waiting, apply paste to additional strips.

USING A WATER BOX
•••

Before hanging a prepasted paper, buy a special plastic container called a water box from your wallpaper dealer. An inexpensive item, it will simplify your job.

Set the box, two-thirds full of water, on newspaper directly below each section of wall as you work. After cutting a strip of wallpaper to the proper length, roll it loosely from bottom to top, with the pattern inside, then lay it in the box to soak for as long as the manufacturer recommends—usually 10 seconds to 1 minute. If the paper floats to the surface, slip an object without sharp edges—such as a wooden dowel—inside the rolled strip to weight it down.

Next, place a stepladder sideways in front of the water box. With the pattern facing you, draw the paper up as you climb the ladder *(above)*. Hang the paper immediately *(pages 82-84)*.

After you have decided on a starting point and established a vertical guideline at that location *(pages 76-79)*, cut the first strip—a length of wallpaper at least 4 inches longer than the height of the wall. At the same time, cut as many additional strips as you plan to hang in one session, making sure that the patterns of successive strips will match. To do this for each new strip, unroll the paper alongside the previously cut strip and shift it up and down until the patterns align *(page 86)*. When you cut the new strip, allow an extra 2 inches at each end.

Apply paste to the strips and let it cure *(pages 80-81)*. If the wallpaper has selvages—blank strips along both edges—remove them after pasting *(Step 1, below)*.

On the Wall: Hang the first strip as explained opposite and on the following page. As you smooth the paper, eliminate air bubbles, especially large ones. The brush strokes that are diagramed on page 84 will take care of most of them. Any small bubbles that resist smoothing will probably vanish as the paper dries. (If some small bubbles persist, you can get rid of them by the tactics described on page 112.)

Trim the strip. Then, before the paste dries, wring a clean sponge in clear water and remove paste from the ceiling, the baseboard, and the face of the strip itself. Rinse the sponge often.

Making Seams: The usual way to join two strips is with a butted seam *(page 87)*; the edges of the wallcovering meet without any overlap. Only in special situations —such as turning corners or allowing for excessive shrinkage—will an overlap be necessary. In such cases, you can opt for either a lapped seam or a less noticeable wire seam, both of which are described on page 87.

Because a vinyl wallcovering will not adhere to itself, you must apply a vinyl-on-vinyl adhesive in order to make an overlapping seam. Alternatively, you can use a technique that is called double-cutting to create a butted seam from an overlap *(page 89)*.

Bonding the Seams: Avoid stretching edges when you join strips of any kind of material. Except for very fragile coverings, use a seam roller to get a strong bond *(page 88)*. Because seam rolling works best after the adhesive has begun to dry, you will save time if you hang four or five strips before starting to roll the seams.

TOOLS

Straightedge	Scissors
Trimming or utility knife	Trimming guide
	Seam roller
Smoothing brush	Sponge

THE FIRST STRIP

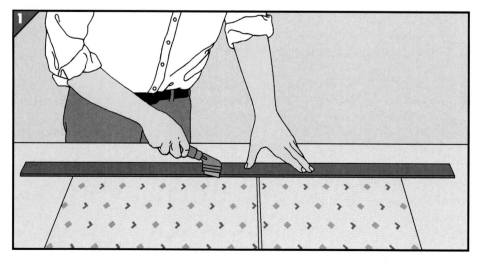

1. Trimming the selvages.
◆ If your paper has selvages, align the side edges of a pasted and folded strip, making sure that the visible portions of the selvages lie precisely over the selvages on the underside of the folds.
◆ Cover the visible selvage on one side with a straightedge. Using the straightedge as a guide, cut off the selvage with a firm, continuous stroke of your trimming knife or any sharp utility knife.
◆ Repeat the procedure on the other side of the strip.

2. Starting the alignment.

◆ Unfold the top section of the strip. Starting at the ceiling line and allowing roughly 2 inches for final trimming along the ceiling, align one of the side edges of the paper with the plumb, or vertical, line.

◆ As you align the paper, pat the top section into place with your hand, just lightly enough to make it hold on the wall. Because pasted wallpaper may stretch, be careful not to pull the edges of the strip.

3. Brushing at the ceiling line.

◆ Brushing with short, upward strokes, press the topmost few inches of paper against the wall, up to—but not beyond—the ceiling line.

◆ Work in this fashion across the entire width of the strip, pressing the paper firmly with the smoothing brush into the angle formed between the ceiling and the wall.

4. Brushing on the top section.

◆ With brisk, light strokes, press the entire top section of the strip against the wall, stopping an inch or so from the upper edge of the lower fold. Do not worry at this stage about occasional air bubbles.

◆ To remove wrinkles, gently pull the lower part of the strip away from the wall up to the point where a wrinkle has formed, then brush the paper smooth.

5. Applying the lower section.

◆ Unfold the lower section of the strip and align it against the plumb line down to the baseboard.

◆ Press this part of the strip to the wall as in Step 4, using light brush strokes and removing wrinkles.

6. Smoothing the strip.

◆ Remove all air bubbles and ensure a firm bond between the paper and the wall with firm brush strokes—using both hands on the brush if necessary. Smooth the paper from the middle of the strip toward its top and bottom edges, following the general direction of the arrows shown at right. Do not move the brush from side to side; this may stretch the paper.

◆ If any wrinkles appear while you are brushing, remove them as you did in Step 4.

◆ Finally, go over the entire surface of the strip with firm, vertical strokes.

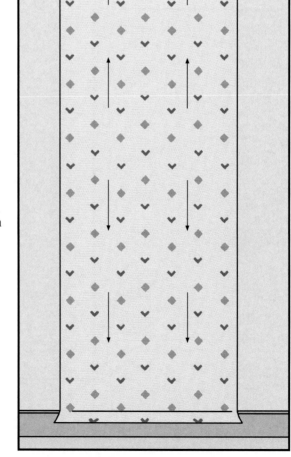

TRIMMING THE STRIPS

1. Creasing the edges.

Press the wallpaper against the upper edge of the baseboard with the blunt side of a pair of scissors. The scissors will form a crease along the line where the paper is to be trimmed.

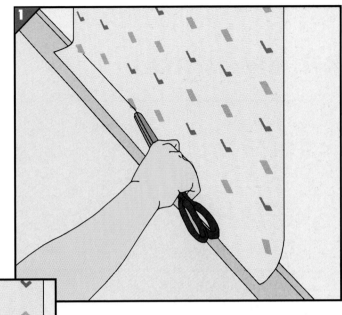

2. Trimming the paper.

◆ Gently lift the strip away from the wall and use scissors to cut off the excess along the crease you made in Step 1 above.

◆ Brush the paper down again with your smoothing brush.

◆ Repeat Steps 1 and 2 along the ceiling line.

Instead of scissors, you can use a trimming knife *(left)* to trim the paper in places where pulling the strip away from the wall would be awkward, such as around windows. Another possibility is a utility knife with snap-off blades *(page 71)*. Be sure to change blades frequently. With either tool, a trimming guide (sold in paint stores) will ensure a straight cutting stroke.

MATCHING PATTERNS

Straight-match pattern.
In this type of pattern, the design stretches across the full width of a strip so that when strips are properly matched the design repeats horizontally from strip to strip. Other designs—such as plaids—may consist of small patterns that repeat horizontally several times between both edges of a strip. In either case, adjacent strips will be identical.

Drop-match pattern.
This type of pattern consists of a design that extends beyond the width of a single strip. The most common variety is drawn in such a way that design elements repeat diagonally on the wall *(left)*. Wallpaper designers usually incorporate a small element of the pattern along the edges of the paper *(arrows)* as a matching guide.

TYPES OF SEAMS

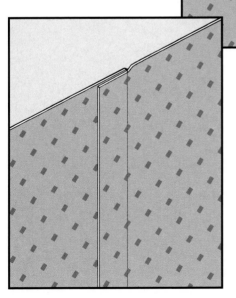

Butted.
For this seam, bring the adjacent edges of two strips of wallpaper firmly against each other until the edges buckle slightly. The buckling eventually flattens out against the wall as the paper dries and shrinks. This is the best-looking seam and the one most frequently employed when papering a flat expanse of wall.

Wire.
The edge of one strip of a wire seam overlaps the adjacent edge by no more than $\frac{1}{16}$ inch, hiding only a tiny portion of the pattern. Use this method if you have trouble butting paper or if the paper shrinks so much that the seams spread open.

Lapped.
In this type of seam, one strip overlaps the adjacent one by $\frac{1}{4}$ to $\frac{1}{2}$ inch. A lapped seam produces a noticeable ridge and is appropriate only in special cases—near corners, for example, where you must correct the alignment of the paper because the walls are not perfectly vertical, or in preparation for double-cutting *(page 89)*.

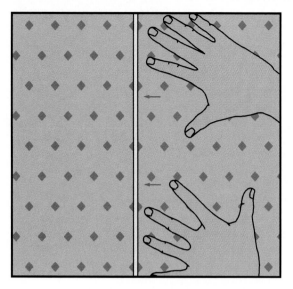

Positioning.

◆ For a butted seam, affix each new strip lightly on the wall about $\frac{1}{4}$ inch away from the previous strip. Keeping your hands flat and well away from the edge of the strip to avoid stretching it, move the strip until the pattern matches and the edges meet and buckle very slightly.

◆ For a lapped seam, affix the strip about $\frac{1}{4}$ inch (or $\frac{1}{16}$ inch for a wire seam) over the previous one instead of away from it. Using the same hand motions, adjust the position of the new strip until the pattern matches.

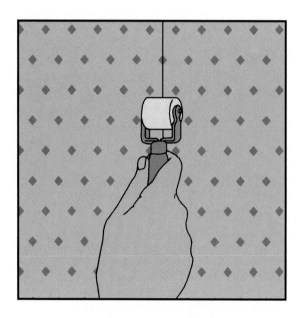

Rolling the seams.

When the adhesive is partly dry—10 to 15 minutes after you have hung a new strip—press the edges of the seam firmly together and against the wall with a seam roller, moving the cylinder against the seam with short up-and-down strokes.

Do not use a seam roller on textured papers, foils, or other fragile coverings; they could be marred by the rolling action. Instead, press the seam with a sponge as shown below.

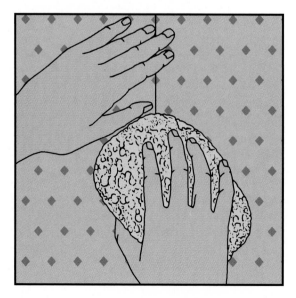

The sponge method.

To join the edges of fragile papers, press each seam gently together with your fingers and a damp sponge.

DOUBLE-CUTTING A LAPPED SEAM

1. Cutting through the seam.
Using a straightedge to guide your trimming knife, slice through both thicknesses of the seam down the middle of the overlap. This will sever two narrow bands of paper, one clearly visible on the outside of the overlap and the other one hidden underneath.

2. Removing the outer band.
Carefully peel off the outer band of the cut overlap. Use your trimming knife to deepen the cut if you find that the separation of the bands is not complete.

3. Removing the inner band.
◆ Lift the edge of the outer strip and peel off the covered band *(left)*.
◆ Press both of the cut edges together with a sponge, and finish with a seam roller *(opposite)*, unless the paper is of a kind that rolling would damage.

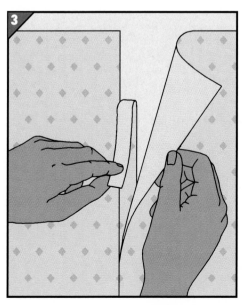

Corners, and the openings and moldings of doors and windows, pose more paperhanging problems than flat walls, but a few simple rules can guide you through the job.

Most corners are at least slightly out of plumb, so a new plumb line is needed on each new stretch of wall *(page 79)*. A less-than-perfect corner can also cause wrinkles if you try to bend more than a few inches of a strip around it. The solution to this and other potential difficulties is to cut the paper lengthwise and hang it in two sections.

Working at Openings: Papering around window moldings *(pages 92-94)*—a technique that you can adapt to doorframes—also requires custom paper-cutting to fit the material to the trim.

A casement window, which is recessed without moldings, is handled by bending the wallpaper into the recess, then finishing with smaller pieces. The exact application method depends on the type of wall covering and the amount of overlap at the opening *(pages 95-99)*. To minimize the effect of unavoidable pattern mismatches, choose a wallcovering with a small overall pattern for a room with casements.

Using a vinyl covering for a casement is trickier than paper, because vinyl cannot adhere to itself in a lapped seam. The seams should be double-cut *(page 89)* and positioned away from casement edges to prevent fraying.

The techniques shown on these and the following pages work from left to right; if you go the other way, simply reverse the directions in the instructions.

TOOLS

Scissors	Sponge	Chalk line
Paste bucket	Water box	Metal straightedge
Paste brush	Trimming knife	Smoothing brushes
	Trimming guide	Seam roller

MATERIALS

Wallcovering
Paste
Water

INNER CORNERS

1. Dividing the strip.
◆ At the top and bottom of the wall, measure the distance between the edge of the last strip and the corner, then add $\frac{1}{2}$ inch to the greater of the two measurements *(right)*.
◆ Use this figure as the width of a partial strip cut from the left side of the paper; save the right-hand section.
◆ Hang the left section next to the last strip, pressing it into the corner and smoothing it onto the adjacent wall. Trim the strip at the top and bottom.

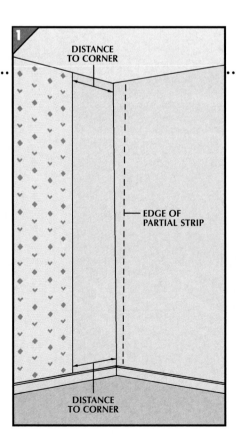

DISTANCE TO CORNER

EDGE OF PARTIAL STRIP

DISTANCE TO CORNER

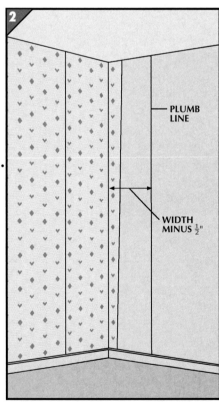

PLUMB LINE

WIDTH MINUS $\frac{1}{2}$"

2. Restoring vertical alignment.
◆ Subtract $\frac{1}{2}$ inch from the width of the right-hand section of the strip.
◆ Measuring from the corner, use this figure to mark the unpapered wall *(above)*, then establish a plumb (vertical) line through the mark *(page 79)*.

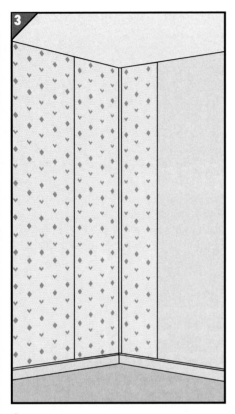

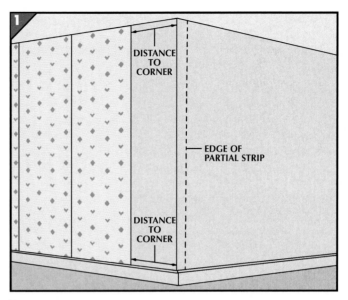

3. Positioning the second piece.

◆ Hang the right-hand section of the split strip with its right edge on the plumb line and its left edge overlapping the first section near the corner.

◆ If you are using a vinyl covering, double-cut the seam *(page 89)*.

The seam or the overlap may slant on the wall because the corner is not plumb (angles exaggerated here for clarity). The resulting visual distortion is usually slight and inconspicuous.

1. Dividing the strip.

◆ At the top and bottom of the wall, measure the distance between the edge of the last strip and the corner, then add 1 inch to the greater of the two measurements *(above)*.

◆ Use the result as the width of a partial strip cut from the left side of the paper; save the right-hand section.

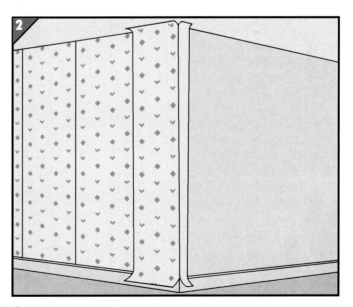

2. Turning the corner.

◆ Hang the left-hand section of the strip, smoothing it on the wall as far as the corner.

◆ Slit the excess paper upward from the ceiling line and downward from the baseboard at the bottom *(above)*.

◆ Fold the paper around the corner and smooth it on the adjacent wall. Trim the strip at the top and at the bottom of both walls.

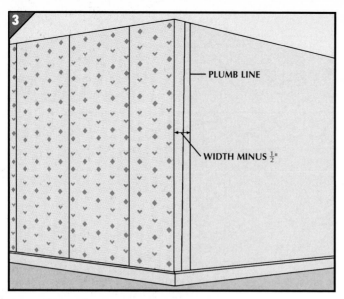

3. Restoring vertical alignment.
◆ Measure the width of the right-hand section of the split strip and subtract ½ inch.
◆ Measuring from the corner, use this figure to mark the unpapered wall *(above)*, then establish a plumb (vertical) line through the mark *(page 79)*.

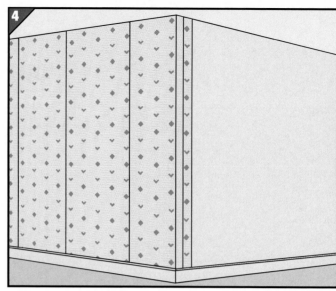

4. Hanging the right-hand section.
Follow the procedure for an inner corner *(page 91, Step 3)*, double-cutting the seam if you are using a vinyl covering.

DOUBLE-HUNG WINDOWS

1. Approaching the window.
◆ Hang the strip that will overlap the left side of the window as you would the preceding strips, but smooth it onto the wall only as far as the window's vertical molding.
◆ Use scissors to cut away any overlap that exceeds 2 inches *(right)*.

2. Slitting the corners.
Cut the paper diagonally at the top and bottom corners of the window molding *(left)*, ending each cut against the wall, precisely where the outer corner of the molding meets the wall.

3. Smoothing the rest of the strip.

◆ Smooth the paper to the wall above and below the window.

◆ Press the wallpaper firmly against the side of the molding.

4. Trimming the strip.

◆ With a trimming knife and a trimming guide, cut away excess paper at the top, side, and bottom of the molding where it meets the wall (above).

◆ When you reach a corner, especially at the sill, make cuts into the trim allowance to ease the tautness of the paper so it will lie flat against the wall.

◆ Trim at the ceiling and baseboard (page 85).

5. Top and bottom strips.

◆ Hang short, full-width strips above and below the window until the distance to the opposite side of the window frame is less than the full width of a strip, matching the pattern carefully.

◆ Trim the strips at the ceiling, the upper and lower moldings, and the baseboard.

6. Attaching the last window strip.

◆ Hang the top of the long strip that overlaps the right side of the window, matching the pattern precisely along the edge of the last short strip.

◆ Smooth the long strip onto the wall only down to the outer corner of the molding.

7. Papering down the second side.

◆ Use scissors to cut a horizontal slit in the paper about 2 inches below the top of the window frame. Stop cutting about 2 inches from the outer edge of the frame. (This cut relieves the pull of the still-unattached portion of the long strip.)
◆ Slit the strip diagonally at the upper corner as was done in Step 2.
◆ Attach the paper along the right side of the window molding, pressing just enough to hold it in place.

8. Matching the last seam.

◆ Trim excess paper and make a diagonal slit at the lower corner.
◆ Slide the left edge of the strip to the edge of the short strip under the window and check the pattern match at the seam.
◆ If the seam is poorly aligned, lift the strip from around the bottom and the side of the window molding, and ease it back into place until the seam at the bottom matches satisfactorily.

9. Finishing the right-hand strip.

◆ With firm strokes of the smoothing brush, smooth the entire strip on the wall, pressing its edges neatly against the molding.
◆ Finish trimming the paper around the side of the window, the ceiling, and along the baseboard.

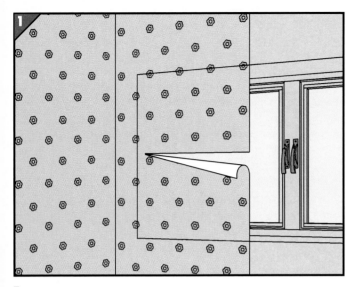

1. The first cut.

◆ Hang the strip of wallpaper that overlaps the casement as you would on a flat wall, pulling it taut and smoothing it on the wall around the recess. Trim excess paper at the ceiling and baseboard.

◆ With scissors, make a horizontal cut in the strip, midway between the top and the bottom of the casement. End the cut about 1 inch from the left side of the casement.

2. Vertical and diagonal cuts.

◆ Cut upward from the end of the horizontal cut, parallel to the casement edge. About 1 inch from the top, cut diagonally to the upper corner of the casement.

◆ Make similar cuts to the lower corner of the casement.

3. Covering the casement.

◆ Brush the upper and lower flaps of wallpaper smoothly onto the top and bottom of the casement recess and trim the paper at the window frame.

◆ Press the paper's narrow vertical flap onto the left edge of the casement.

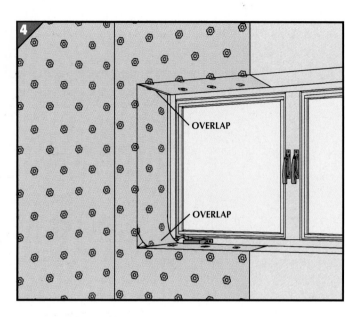

4. Completing the job.

◆ Measure and cut a matching piece as wide as the side of the recess and long enough to overlap the flaps on the top and bottom.

◆ Hang the piece on the side and smooth it against the side, top, and bottom.

To finish papering the casement, hang short full-width strips above and below as needed, then repeat the steps shown here to cover the other side.

CASEMENT WINDOWS AND VINYL COVERINGS—LONG OVERLAP

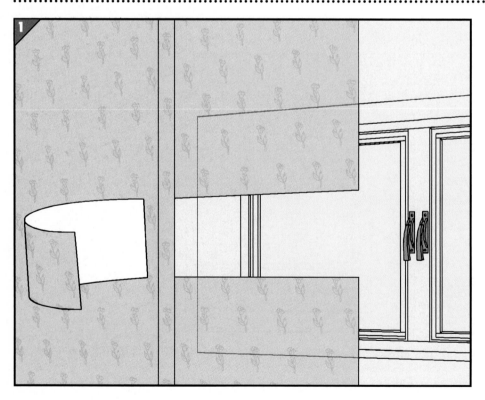

1. The first cut.

◆ When most of a strip of vinyl wallpaper overlaps a casement window, hang it as on a flat wall, smooth it, and trim it at the ceiling and baseboard.

◆ Cut out a full-width section of the strip in the middle of the opening, leaving enough paper above and below to cover the top and bottom of the recess. Make the cuts with scissors over the recess; use a trimming knife over the wall.

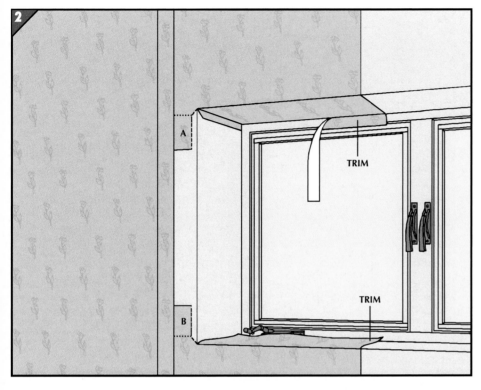

2. Hanging the overlap.

◆ Starting at the top and bottom corners of the casement, slit the vinyl on the wall with a trimming knife, making two cuts, each at a 45-degree angle and about $1\frac{1}{2}$ inches long. Then make two vertical cuts from the ends of these diagonals to the edges of the section you have removed. (These four cuts are indicated by dashed lines in the drawing at left.)

◆ From 1 inch below and above the ends of the diagonal cuts, make two horizontal cuts to the left edge of the strip (*dotted lines*) and pull away the two rectangles of paper marked A and B.

◆ Press and smooth the overlapping flaps onto the top and bottom of the casement, then trim them at the window frame.

3. Completing the job.

◆ Cut a piece of wallpaper as long as the height of the casement and that matches the pattern on the strip to the left of the window. Trim the piece to a width that will reach from the last complete strip around the corner to the window frame—plus a 4-inch allowance for trimming and double-cut joints.

◆ Paste and hang this piece, and trim it at the window frame. Along the left, top, and bottom edges of the piece, double-cut the overlaps (*page 89*).

Finish papering the casement by hanging short full-width strips above and below as needed, then repeat the steps shown here to cover the other side.

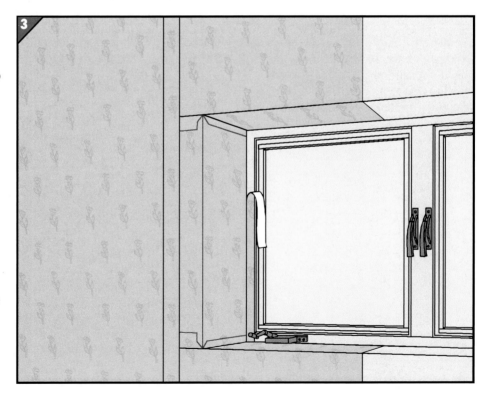

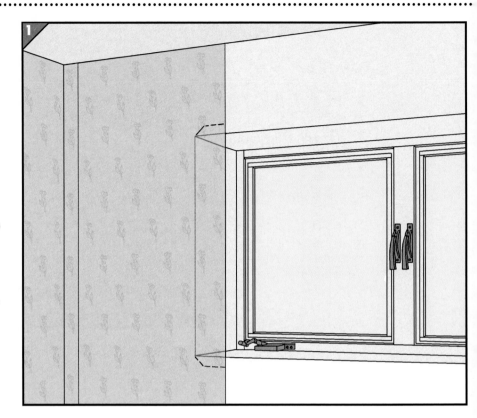

1. The first cuts.

◆ When a strip of vinyl wallpaper overlaps only a few inches of a casement window, hang it as on a flat wall and trim it at the ceiling and the baseboard.

◆ At the top and bottom corners of the casement, use a trimming knife to make two 45-degree cuts along the wall, each about $1\frac{1}{2}$ inches long, above and below the casement *(dashed lines, right)*. Continue the cuts parallel to the top and bottom of the casement.

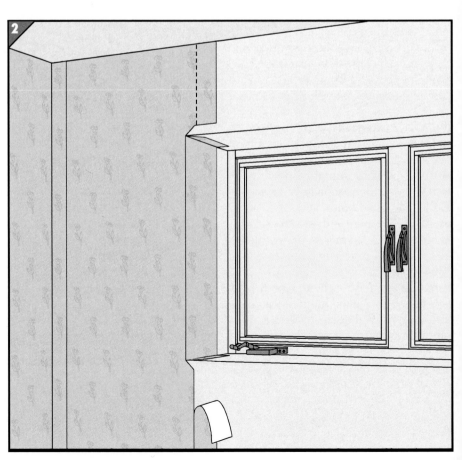

2. Hanging the flap.

◆ Press and smooth the flap onto the side of the casement, pasting the projections at the flap's ends to the top and bottom of the casement recess.

◆ Starting at the ends of the diagonal cuts, make vertical cuts to the ceiling and baseboard. Pull off and discard the narrow lengths of paper above and below the casement.

3. Fitting the matching piece.

◆ Measure and cut a piece of wallpaper, matching the pattern of the flap, the same length as the flap and about 1 inch wider than the distance from the edge of the flap to the window frame.

◆ Paste and hang the matching piece flush with the window frame, then double-cut *(page 89)* along the overlap between the flap and the new piece.

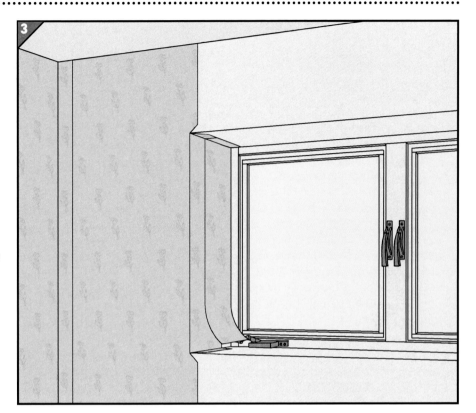

4. Hanging the next strip.

◆ Cut a matching section of wallpaper long enough to cover the wall above the casement and the top surface of the casement recess—plus a 4-inch trim allowance.

◆ Paste and hang the strip flush with the left edge of the casement, and trim it at the ceiling and the window frame.

◆ Cover the area from the bottom of the frame to the baseboard with another matching section.

◆ Double-cut all overlaps between the new strip, the previous strip, and the matching piece on the casement side.

Finish papering the casement by hanging short full-width strips above and below as needed. Repeat the steps shown here to cover the other side.

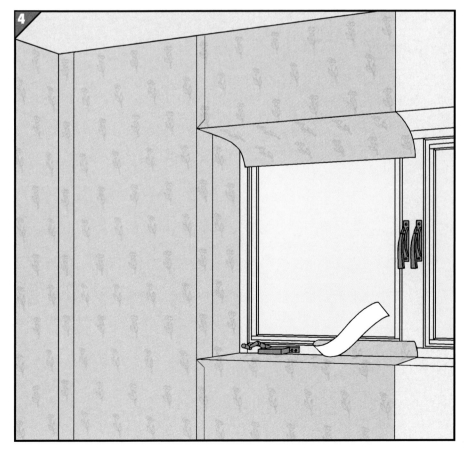

The high walls of a stairway, the slanted walls of a dormer room, and an arched doorway require special techniques for handling long strips of paper and for papering along angles and around curves.

Planning and Strategy: Prepare all surfaces thoroughly *(pages 72-75)*. Estimate the amount of paper needed for stairwell walls *(page 115)*, and buy at least one extra roll to allow for trimming the slanting bottoms of the strips. Measure and cut the strips for the wall beside the stairs, called the well wall, one by one to be sure that each is the correct length.

Slanted walls and their unusual angles present special problems. Estimate the amount of paper needed by measuring the area of all the surfaces to be covered as accurately

as possible, then add at least one extra roll to compensate for the oddly shaped sections you will cut. Paper a recessed, walk-in dormer separately, rather than as part of the main room.

When papering an archway, measure around the opening, floor to floor, with a tape measure, and allow an extra 2 inches to account for overlaps and slight imperfections in the arch that cannot be measured by the tape.

Use vinyl-to-vinyl adhesive when overlapping corners with vinyl wall coverings, or use the double-cutting technique shown on page 89.

Choosing a Paper: For all these jobs, a small, scattered pattern is better than a large, bold design; precise matching is almost impossible with long, cumbersome strips in

a stairwell, and with such a pattern slight mismatches are less noticeable. The same is true for slanted walls, where a scattered pattern would help disguise the inevitable mismatches that result where angled walls meet.

When papering an arch choose a pattern without a strong up-and-down orientation. Doing so makes it easier to match the pattern on the inside of the arch and prevents the paper from appearing to be upside down across the top of the arch.

⚠️ *Be sure to observe the rules of ladder safety described* **CAUTION** *on pages 8 to 11. If the ceiling height of the upper floor is more than 8 feet, do not use the improvised scaffold shown here; instead, rent scaffolding and have it set up by a professional.*

TOOLS

Stepladder	Smoothing brush	Paste brush and bucket
Extension ladder	Seam roller	Water box
Scaffold-grade plank	Tape measure	Plumb bob
(2 x 10)	Utility knife	Trimming knife

HANDLING THE HEIGHTS OF A STAIRWELL

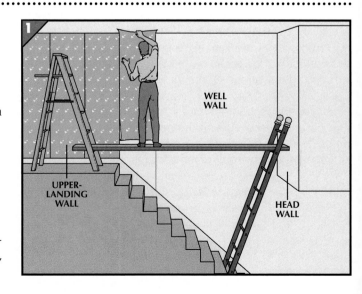

1. Hanging the top of the first strip.
◆ Set up a platform for the stairwell *(page 10),* then mark a plumb line at the point where the baseboard angles downward *(page 79).*
◆ Paper the upper-landing wall *(pages 82-85),* aligning the right side of the first strip on the plumb line.
◆ Mark another plumb line one strip width to the right of the first plumb line. Prepare a strip of paper the length of this line plus 4 inches for top and bottom allowances.
◆ Working from the platform, hang the top of the first well-wall strip. Overlap the strip onto the ceiling about 2 inches, and butt it against the adjacent upper-landing strip.

WELL WALL

UPPER-LANDING WALL

HEAD WALL

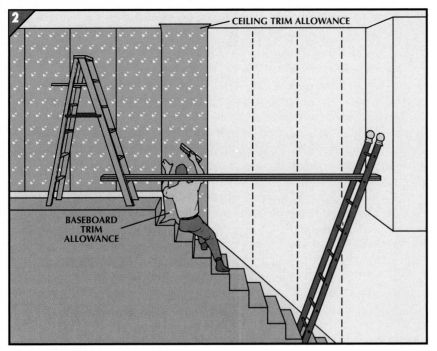

2. Finishing the bottom of the strip.

◆ Unfold and hang the bottom section of the first well-wall strip.

◆ Finish smoothing the top section. Crease and trim the paper at the ceiling line *(page 85),* and then roll the seam halfway down the strip.

◆ Smooth the bottom section. Crease and trim the paper along the baseboard; then roll the rest of the seam and smooth the entire strip.

◆ Hang the remaining well-wall strips *(dashed lines)* by the same method until you have hung the last full-width strip before the corner between the well wall and the head wall.

3. Turning the inner corner.

◆ Measure from the edge of the last strip to the head wall and add $\frac{1}{2}$ inch. Cut a strip lengthwise this distance from its left edge.

◆ Hang the top of this section, making a 1-inch slit at the top corner and smoothing the $\frac{1}{2}$-inch overlap onto the head wall.

◆ Crease and trim the paper at the ceiling line and roll the seam as far as you can. If possible, work from the staircase when applying the middle of this long section; otherwise, arrange the platform as shown in Step 5.

◆ Continue applying and smoothing the section downward, and make a $\frac{1}{2}$-inch slit where the bottom of the head wall meets the well wall. Press the paper below the slit against the well wall, and trim it at the bottom.

◆ Measure the width of the remaining section of the strip you cut lengthwise and subtract $\frac{1}{2}$ inch. Mark a plumb line on the head wall that distance from the corner between the well wall and head wall.

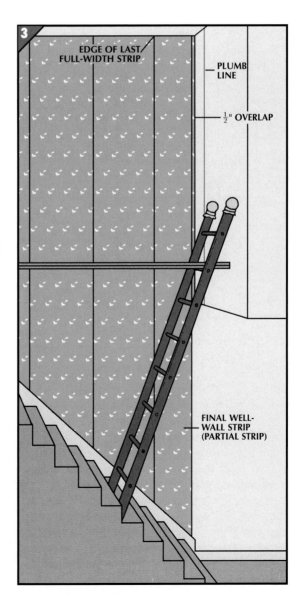

FIRST HEAD-WALL STRIP (PARTIAL STRIP)

PLUMB LINE

4. Papering the head wall.

◆ Measure the height of the head wall, excluding any moldings. To the height add 4 inches for top and bottom trim allowances; cut both the remaining section of the corner strip and the other full-width strips for the head wall to this length.

◆ Paste and fold the remaining section of the corner strip, hanging the top only and aligning its right edge to the plumb line.

◆ Hang the tops of the remaining strips until you reach the last full-width strip before the far corner.

◆ Cut a partial strip lengthwise for the far corner. The overlap will vary: For an outer corner, as shown in the drawing, add 1 inch; an inner corner requires only $\frac{1}{2}$ inch.

◆ Hang the top of this last strip, slitting the top of the paper so it fits around the corner.

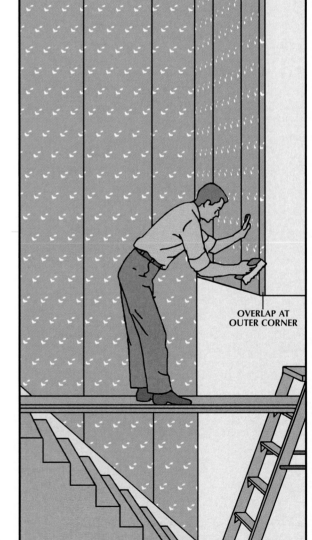

SLIT

OVERLAP AT OUTER CORNER

5. Completing the job.

◆ Arrange the stairwell platform so that you can comfortably reach the bottom of the head wall *(right)*, then hang the bottoms of the strips.

◆ Smooth the overlap around the corner, slitting the paper at the bottom corner. When the strips are in place, press out bubbles and smooth the paper with a clean paint roller on a long handle or with a broom covered with a clean rag.

◆ Trim the bottoms of the strips flush with the bottom of the head wall, treating a molding there as if it were a baseboard.

◆ Reassemble the two-ladder platform and trim the strips at the ceiling line.

◆ If the stairwell has three sides, or another inner corner, go on to paper the second well wall, and then paper the remaining landing walls.

COVERING SLANTED WALLS

1. Hanging the top of the corner.

◆ Hang vertical strips of paper as described on pages 82 to 85.
◆ Where a strip first overlaps the slanted corner, crease the paper along the ceiling line as far as possible, then make a small slit in the paper where the ceiling meets the top of the slanted corner so the paper lies flat. Crease the paper into the corner.
◆ Trim at the ceiling line as far as the corner, then cut the rest of the strip parallel to the corner, leaving a $\frac{1}{2}$-inch overlap.
◆ For the remaining full-width strips, measure the right-hand edge of the preceding strip from corner to baseboard and add 4 inches. Hang the strips, creasing each into the slanted corner before trimming, to leave a $\frac{1}{2}$-inch overlap on the slanted wall.

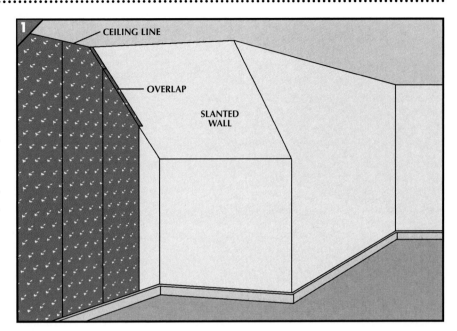

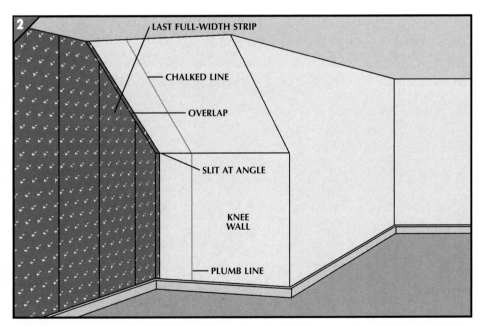

2. Finishing the corner.

◆ Measure the horizontal distance from the edge of the last full-width strip to the corner of the short vertical wall—called a knee wall—and add $\frac{1}{2}$ inch to this measurement. Find the vertical distance from the top of the last full-width strip's right-hand edge to the baseboard, then add 4 inches for trim allowances.
◆ Cut a partial strip as wide as the first figure and as long as the second. Hang the strip, butting its left edge against the last full-width strip.

◆ Crease and trim the top of the strip against the slanted wall, leaving a $\frac{1}{2}$-inch overlap for turning the corner. Make a slit at the angle between the slanted wall and the knee wall, and another slit at the baseboard. Trim all the strips flush to the baseboard.
◆ To mark the position for the first strip on the slanted and knee walls, measure the width of your wallpaper and subtract $\frac{1}{2}$ inch. Mark a plumb line on the knee wall this distance from the corner. Using the same measurement, snap a chalk line on the slanted wall.

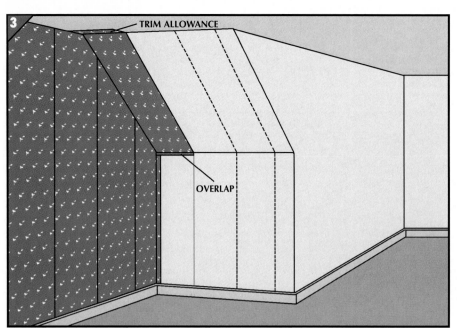

TRIM ALLOWANCE

OVERLAP

3. Covering the slanted and knee walls.

◆ Measure the distance between the ceiling and the joint where the slanted and knee walls meet, and add $2\frac{1}{2}$ inches. Cut a full-width strip to this length.
◆ Measure the height of the knee wall, and add 2 inches. Cut a second full-width strip of paper to this length.
◆ Hang the right edge of the first strip along the chalked line on the slanted wall, with $\frac{1}{2}$ inch of overlap onto the knee wall. Align and hang the second strip along the plumb line of the knee wall, covering the $\frac{1}{2}$-inch overlap.
◆ Smooth the strips, then trim the al-

lowances at the ceiling and baseboard.
◆ Hang full widths of paper *(dashed lines)* up to the last full-width strips before the corner.
◆ If the slanted wall and knee wall end at an outer corner, proceed to Steps 4 and 5.
◆ For an inner corner, such as is found with a walk-in dormer, paper the facing wall using the same techniques that are described in Steps 1 and 2, overlapping the paper onto the slanted and knee walls.
◆ Then measure the distance from the last full-width strip to the corner and hang a strip of that size, covering the overlaps on the slanted and knee walls.

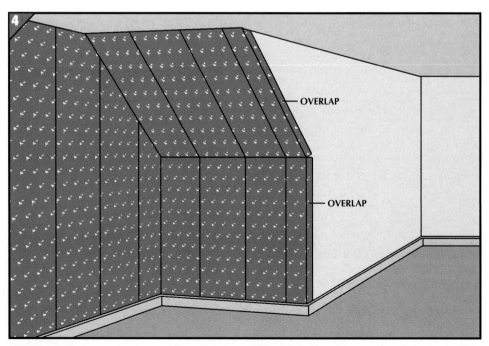

OVERLAP

OVERLAP

4. Turning an outer corner.

◆ Measure the distance from the edge of the last full-width strips to the outer corner, and add 1 inch. Use this figure for the width of partial strips for the slanted and knee walls, making them as long as the strips cut for Step 3.

◆ Cut and hang these final strips separately, and slit the paper at the ceiling and at the baseboard to fit it around the corner.
◆ Before tackling the triangular sections next to the slanted wall, hang the remaining full vertical strips.

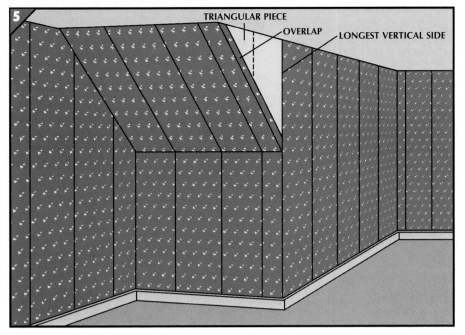

5. Papering leftover triangles.
◆ First measure and cut paper for the longest vertical side of the triangle, including trim allowances and using the full width of the paper if possible. Hang the strip, then trim it to fit—in this case, horizontally at the ceiling and diagonally at the outer corner.
◆ Measure the small triangle to the left of the last strip, then hang a piece of wallpaper cut to this size and shape, plus trim allowances.

Labels in illustration: TRIANGULAR PIECE, OVERLAP, LONGEST VERTICAL SIDE

PAPERING AN ARCH

Getting around the curve.
◆ Paper the wall in which the arch is built, allowing the wall covering to extend 1 inch into the opening.
◆ Make relief cuts every 3 or 4 inches *(inset)*, stopping $\frac{1}{8}$ inch from the edge of the opening. Wrap the resulting flaps around the corner, rewetting the paste if necessary.
◆ Let the paste dry, then trim the flaps $\frac{1}{8}$ inch from the edge of the opening.
◆ Cut two side strips of wallpaper equal in width to the thickness of the arch wall and long enough to reach from the baseboard to a point where the arch be-

gins to curve. Hang one piece on each side of the archway.
◆ Cut a center strip 2 inches longer than the distance between the tops of the side strips, and hang it, overlapping the side strips.
◆ Double-cut the seams *(page 89)*.

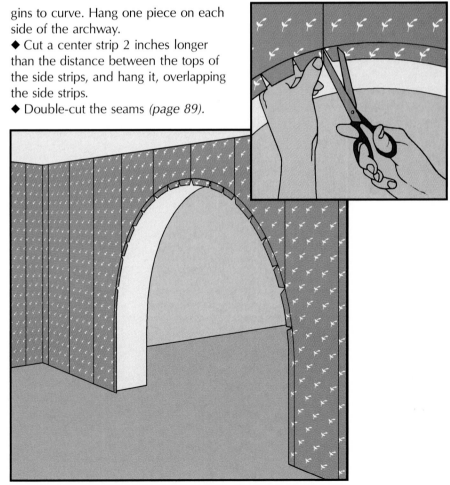

Switch Plates and Other Obstacles

When hanging wallpaper, the best way to deal with a fixture is not to paper around it but to remove the obstacle and paper under it. After the fixture has been restored to its place, it will appear to rest against a surface design unbroken by any seam.

For a receptacle or, as shown here, a light switch, you need only detach a cover plate. For a wall-hung lamp, you must detach the fixture and also disconnect its wires.

⚠️ **CAUTION** *Never dismantle an electrical fix-ture without first removing the fuse or tripping the circuit breaker that controls current to it. This precaution is especially important in paperhanging: Wet wallpaper adhesive is an excellent conductor of electricity and can create a dangerous shock hazard.*

TOOLS

Voltage tester
Screwdriver
Trimming knife
Scissors

1. Detaching the plate.
◆ Turn off power to the switch.
◆ Undo the screws in the cover plate, and remove the plate.
◆ Check the switch with a voltage tester to make sure it is off.

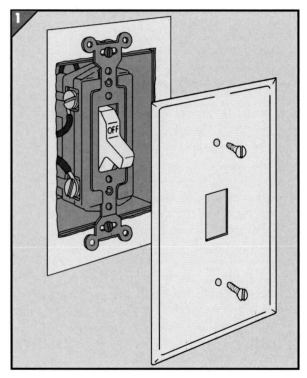

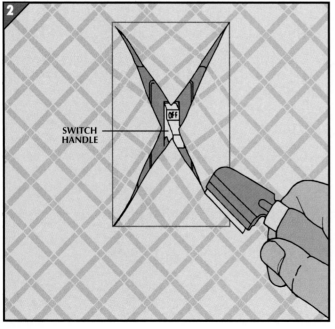

SWITCH HANDLE

2. Cutting a hole for the switch.
◆ Hang a strip of wallpaper in the usual manner, covering the recessed box.
◆ Split a small opening to uncover the switch handle, and with a trimming knife or scissors, cut diagonally to each corner of the box (*left*).
◆ Cut the flaps of the X to make a rectangular hole as big as the box, using the inside of the box as a guide.
◆ Screw the plate back on—perhaps first covering it with matching paper (*Steps 3-5*).

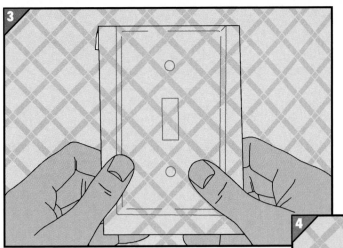

3. Matching the paper for the cover plate.

◆ Cut a piece of paper larger than the plate.
◆ Slip the plate over its switch, ease the plate's top away from the wall, and fold the top of the paper over the plate. Match the upper fold of the paper to the wall above.

4. Allowing for the bevels.

◆ If the paper on the plate matches that on the wall perfectly at the top but poorly at the bottom because of the beveled shape of the plate, create a close match at both edges by moving the paper about $\frac{1}{8}$ inch downward *(arrow)*.
◆ Fold the top and bottom of the paper over the plate, and crease these folds firmly.
◆ To match the side edges, follow the same procedure: Fold one side of the paper over the plate, match the pattern at this edge of the plate, then move the paper about $\frac{1}{8}$ inch away from the edge.
◆ Fold the paper over the left and right edges of the plate, and crease these folds firmly.

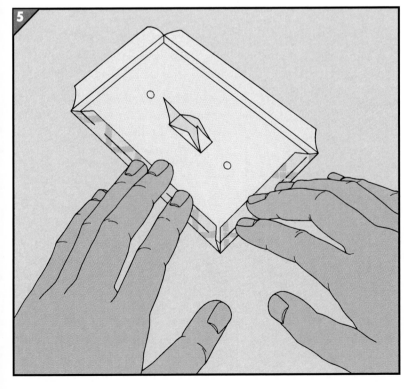

5. Covering the plate.

◆ Apply adhesive to the matching piece of paper, and mount it on the front of the plate, using the creases you have made as a guide for exact placement.
◆ Cut off the corners of the paper diagonally with a pair of scissors, then fold the paper over the back of the plate and press it firmly to both sides of the plate.
◆ Cut a small X over the switch-handle slot of the plate, and fold the flaps through the slot to the back of the plate.
◆ Mark the location of the screw holes, and remount the plate.

Borders are narrow strips of wall covering used to highlight elements of a room. Applied over paint or wallpaper, borders can frame mirrors or pictures and accent the edges of windows and doors. Often, a border circles an entire room, either at chair-rail height—36 to 40 inches above the floor—or along the wall where it meets the ceiling.

Border Basics: Borders are sold prepasted in 5-yard spools or, in some cases, by the yard. Measure the path the border is to cover. Add 10 percent to the total to account for waste resulting from matching the pattern at seams or making miter cuts around corners of doors, windows, and the like *(opposite)*.

When applying a border over paint, follow the wall-preparation techniques described on page 72. If you are pasting the strip to a wall covering, you will need to brush on

a vinyl-to-vinyl adhesive after soaking the paper to moisten the paste.

To prevent the pattern of a dark wall covering from showing through a light-colored border, apply an opaque primer-sealer to mask the underlying pattern *(page 72)*. To do so, lightly mark the border area in pencil, then carefully coat the wall covering within the outline.

Begin hanging the border in an inconspicuous corner in case you cannot make a perfect match where the end of the border meets the beginning. Elsewhere, butt border segments together if the pattern match is acceptable. If not, overlap the pieces until you achieve a match, then double-cut the seam *(page 89)*. Turn corners using the techniques for regular wallpaper *(pages 90-92)*.

Other Considerations: Carefully mark with a level guideline the

route that the border will follow. A border hung even slightly askew at one end will slant noticeably as it crosses the wall.

Choose a nondirectional pattern if the border will be applied both horizontally and vertically. Make sure that elements such as mirrors or pictures that you want to accent have square corners; if they do not, hanging a border will only emphasize the irregularity.

TOOLS

Tape measure
Carpenter's level
Water box
Paste brush and
  bucket

Smoothing brush
Combination
  square
Utility knife
Straightedge
Seam roller

HORIZONTAL BORDERS

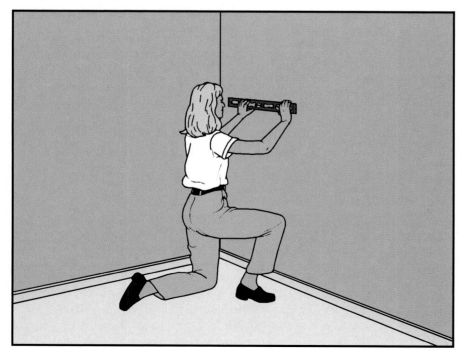

Plotting a level line.

Because floors and ceilings sometimes are not level, do not rely on measurements that use them as reference points. Instead, make a series of horizontal tick marks on the wall for the top edge of the border with a pencil and a carpenter's level to maintain a consistently level line across a wall.

Preparing a border.
◆ Cut the border to manageable lengths—4 to 6 feet—and roll each loosely with the pattern facing inside.
◆ Immerse the rolls in water one at a time for the period recommended by the manufacturer.
◆ Unroll the border and apply vinyl-to-vinyl adhesive. Then fold the paper into a series of 6-inch pleats, paste side to paste side, with the edges aligned and without creasing the folds *(left)*.
◆ Allow the paper to "rest" for the time recommended by the manufacturer before applying the border to the wall.

MITERING CORNERS

1. Applying the first leg.
◆ Paste the first strip along an edge of a window sill—the bottom, in this case—so that the ends extend beyond the corners by at least one full width of the border.
◆ Remove any wrinkles and bubbles from this strip with a smoothing brush before hanging the next section—here, along the side of the window.

COMBINATION SQUARE

WASTE PIECES

2. Cutting the miter.
◆ Match the pattern of the two strips at the inside of the corner, smoothing the strip as you position it.
◆ Lightly mark a 45-degree line from the corner of the window to the outside edges of the borders, setting a combination square against the window frame as a guide *(left)*.
◆ Cut through both layers of border, and peel away the two waste pieces that result.
◆ Smooth the strips against the wall, and roll the seam.

Wallpaper is vulnerable to a variety of small flaws or injuries, but it is also easily repaired. For example, to secure a loose seam or a tear whose flap is intact, simply paste the paper down again, using a small, long-handled artist's brush to apply the adhesive so that the paper is not stretched. Other fixes are only slightly more complicated.

Patching Holes: The torn-patch method shown below produces an almost invisible repair for holes no larger than about an inch. This technique works best on light paper with a small, busy pattern. The double-cut method described on the opposite page serves for larger holes or dark papers. It must be used for vinyls and foils, which cannot be torn.

Deflating Bubbles: If bubbles are inconspicuous or located out of harm's way, leave them alone. However, if they are located in a place where an accidental puncture could result in a tear, flatten them as explained on pages 112 to 113.

TOOLS

Artist's brush
Metal straightedge
Utility knife
Putty knife
Sponge

MATERIALS

Wallpaper paste
Masking tape

THE TORN-PATCH METHOD

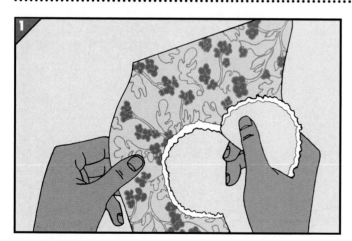

1. Tearing a neat patch.
◆ Practice tearing on a scrap of the same or similar wallpaper before you make the patch. Grasp the paper with the index finger of one hand atop the section that will be the patch, and the thumb of the other hand atop the section that will be discarded.
◆ Rotate the hand holding the patch section gently upward *(above)* and twist it slightly in toward the other hand; at the same time, pull down and toward the patch with the other hand. This should produce a patch with an intact design on top and a feathered edge on the underside. The entire patch should be no more than 3 inches wide.

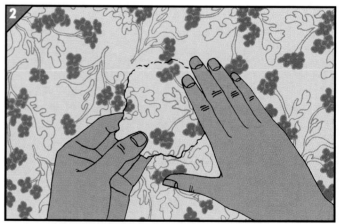

2. Applying the patch.
◆ If you use adhesive, apply a thin layer to the patch with an artist's brush, stroking outward from the center to the feathered edge. For prepasted paper, wet the patch and shake off excess water.
◆ Handle the fragile edge carefully as you position the patch over the damaged paper, and match the top of the patch to the pattern below.
◆ Make the final pattern alignment when the whole piece is in place. The match may not be exact, but the discrepancy is rarely great enough to be noticeable.

THE DOUBLE-CUT METHOD

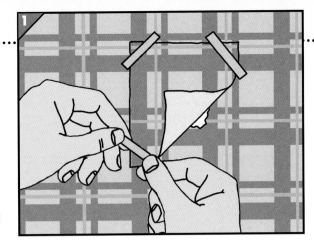

1. Placing the patch.

◆ Cut a scrap that overlaps the damaged area by about 1 inch on all sides. If the damage is located in one corner of a pattern square, as in the example shown, the patch should include the whole square.

◆ Position the wallpaper scrap over the damaged area, align it to the pattern exactly, and secure it with masking tape (right).

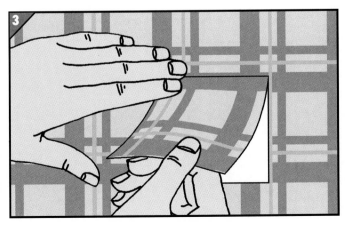

2. Making the cut.

◆ Hold a metal straightedge against one side of the scrap piece. With a sharp utility knife, cut cleanly through both layers of paper—along pattern lines, if possible—all around the damaged section (left).

◆ Carefully peel off the masking tape and remove the patch and the scrap that it was cut from. If any part of the patch is still attached to the scrap, place the paper on a work surface and neatly cut the pieces apart with the knife.

◆ Go over the cuts on the damaged section of wallpaper with the utility knife to make sure that the edges have been completely separated.

◆ Pry up one corner of the cut area with the tip of the blade. With vinyls and most heavy papers, it should come out in one piece. If it does not, pry gently all around the edge with a putty knife (inset). Then scrape any glue or lumps of paper off the wall.

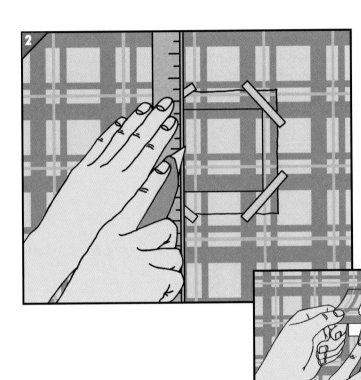

3. Inserting the patch.

◆ If you use adhesive, apply it to the wall with a small artist's brush in order to avoid smearing any on the undamaged wallpaper. If your paper is prepasted, wet the patch and shake off the excess water.

◆ Hold the patch lightly with the fingers of both hands, taking care not to crease the paper. Insert the top edge into the cleaned-out section (left), pat it down lightly, then let the rest of the patch fall into place and press it gently with a clean, damp sponge.

◆ After a few minutes press again with a clean sponge to be sure the patch is firmly in place and that all corners and edges are down.

CUTTING FLAPS TO FLATTEN A BUBBLE

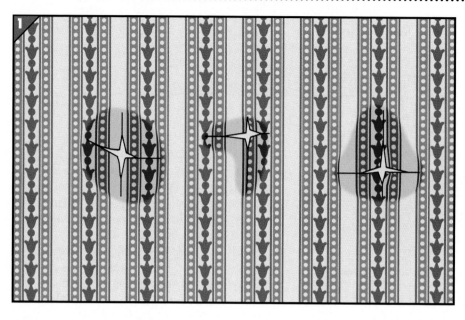

1. Making the cuts.

Most bubbles can be eliminated by making two crosswise cuts, which let air escape and create flaps so that adhesive can be applied to the underside of the paper. Bubbles pop up in a variety of shapes, three of which are shown by shaded areas in the drawing, along with the best configuration of cuts to make for each shape. Slash along a pattern line wherever possible.

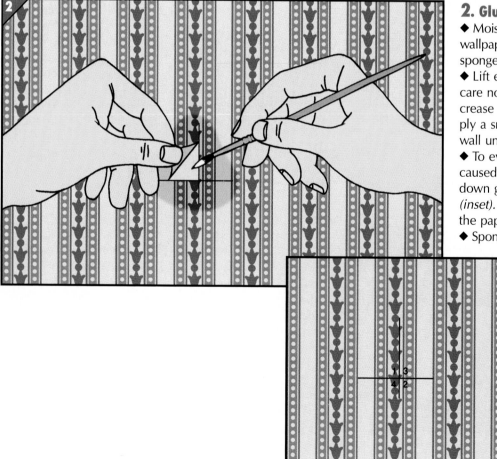

2. Gluing down the flaps.

◆ Moisten the patterned side of the wallpaper flaps with a clean, damp sponge to make them flexible.

◆ Lift each flap in turn, taking special care not to bend it back far enough to crease it. With a thin artist's brush, apply a small amount of adhesive to the wall underneath.

◆ To evenly distribute any slack caused by stretching, pat the flaps down gently in the sequence indicated *(inset)*. Any overlap will disappear as the paper dries and shrinks.

◆ Sponge off excess adhesive after the flaps have been in place for a few minutes, but take care not to raise the flaps with the sponge.

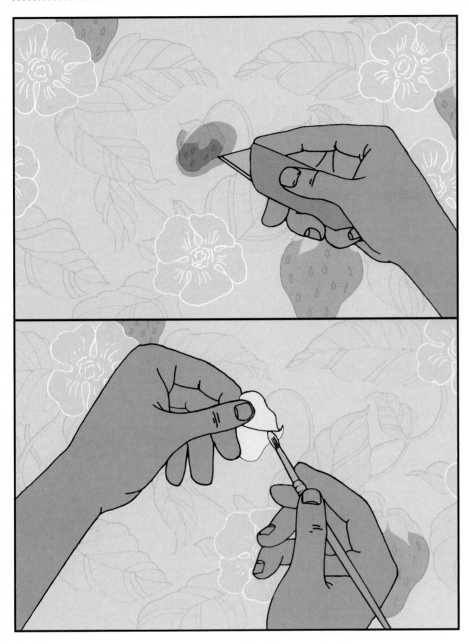

Cutting on a curve.

On some wallpaper patterns, such as the one that is shown above, a bubble can be flattened by making one curved cut instead of two intersecting slashes. The bubble *(shaded area)* in this wallpaper has developed directly under a circular pattern design. When this situation or a similar one occurs, make a single curved cut that is three-quarters of the way around the edge of the design and coinciding with the pattern. Lift, without creasing, the curved flap that you have cut, then paste down the flap as described in Step 2 on page 112.

Most of today's wall coverings can be washed with mild soap and water. Never use abrasive powdered cleansers on wallpaper, even vinyls, and never use household cleaners containing kerosene or other petroleum distillates.

Start at the bottom of a wall and work upward: If you work from the top, the dirty water will flow down onto the dirt-clogged paper, leaving streaks that are very hard to remove. When the dirt is off, rinse the paper with clean water.

The material called cleaning dough, which works like a big eraser, is ideal for surfaces that are not washable. Stubborn spots that will not come off with the dough can often be removed with a paste made from carbon tetrachloride and cornstarch or fuller's earth; when the paste has dried, brush it away. Before using cleaning dough or the paste, make a test application in an inconspicuous area; either cleaner could change the paper's appearance.

Clear protective-spray coatings render any wallpaper washable and add special protection over patched areas. Apply these coatings as soon as the adhesive is dry under the paper and before dust has a chance to build up.

For future repairs, save unused powdered adhesive and wallpaper scraps. Label the adhesive container and put it in a cool, dry place. Store leftover scraps in a sheet of brown wrapping paper sealed in a cardboard mailing tube.

Appendix

No single wall coating or covering is right for every situation. Paints, primers, stains, and sealers must be chosen based on the surface they will cover. Wallpaper must meet somewhat different criteria for appearance, durability, and ease of removal. Consult the guides on the following pages to select—and buy the right amount of—the best interior or exterior coating or wall covering for your needs.

ESTIMATING QUANTITIES

INTERIOR PAINT

To estimate the amount of paint you will need for a job, first calculate the area to be painted *(below)*. Next, divide the result by the area that a gallon of paint will cover—400 square feet of previously painted wallboard or plaster, 350 square feet of textured or previously unpainted walls. When applying a light color over a dark one—or vice versa—two coats may be needed. For the second coat, use a figure of 450 square feet per gallon on a smooth-surface wall and 400 square feet per gallon for a rough wall. Estimate the amount of trim paint you will need in the same way.

WALLPAPER

To calculate the amount of wallpaper necessary to cover a room, first find the room's area *(below)*. Wall coverings are measured in units called single rolls. Though the width of papers may range from 15 to 54 inches, a single roll contains approximately 28 to 30 square feet of covering. Expect to waste about 3 to 5 square feet per single roll on odd-shaped areas, on points where the wall ends before your pattern does, and in trimming excess paper from the top and bottom of a strip. Therefore, divide your total wall area by 25 square feet to find the number of single-roll units you will need. Don't underbuy; wallpaper is printed in dye lots that might be difficult or impossible to match later.

Calculating Area

For a rectangular room *(right)*, measure the length and width, round up each figure to the nearest foot, and add them together. Multiply that total by the wall height—measured from baseboard to ceiling or top molding—and double that result. Subtract doors and windows, allowing 21 square feet for each door and 15 square feet for an average window. The final figure is the wall area in square feet. If the room is an unusual shape, measure the height and width of each wall section. Then multiply each set of figures, and add the products for the total wall area.

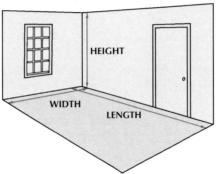

Ceiling area is the length times the width of the room. Measure and figure trim and door areas separately, especially if you are using a different color or type of paint.

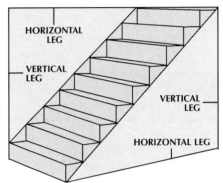

A stairwell *(above)* often forms a triangular shape. For the area of a triangle, multiply the length of the horizontal leg by the length of the vertical leg and divide by two.

EXTERIOR PAINT

To calculate the amount of paint to buy for the exterior of a house, you will need to know its perimeter and height. Measure the perimeter of your house in segments. For a rough estimate of the height, figure 10 feet for each story and add 2 feet if your house has gables. Or count the number of courses of clapboards or shingles and multiply by the height of a single course. Multiply the perimeter of the house by its height. Subtract from this figure the area of doors (approximately 21 square feet each) and windows (approximately 15 square feet each for the average size). Then divide the resulting figure by the number of square feet that 1 gallon of your paint will cover. The result will be the total paint requirement for one coat applied with a brush or roller. If you plan to spray-paint your house *(pages 66-67)*, you may have to double your paint order, since a sprayer applies the equivalent of two coats of paint at once.

To estimate the amount of outside trim paint needed, measure one shutter or door (or one of each size if they vary) and multiply that area by the number of shutters or doors on your house. Then measure and add in the trim around each door and window. If you intend to paint gutters, assume that each foot of length represents a square foot of area: for example, if you have 60 feet of metal gutter along your eaves, buy enough trim paint to cover 60 square feet.

Not all paints are compatible with every surface. Alkyd-base paints, for example, are the wrong coating for fresh plaster; as the plaster dries, moisture and salts migrate to the surface and push paint away. A better choice in this case would be latex-base paint, which breathes better than alkyds.

Furthermore, the wrong paint can actually damage a surface. Latex paint, which is thinned with water, promotes rust if it is applied directly to iron or steel. And the thinners in other coatings may dissolve glue; if paint containing such a solvent is used over wallpaper, both paper and paint could peel right off the wall.

The chart on these pages is intended to help you avoid such errors. To learn more about these finishes—what they are made of, what kind of preparations they require, how fast they dry—turn to pages 118 to 121 for interior coatings and pages 122 to 123 for exterior ones.

Some of the materials listed on this chart can be found on both the inside and outside of a house. Therefore, the paints compatible with these surfaces are usually available in interior and exterior formulations. Never paint an exterior with interior paint; it cannot expand and contract with the temperature and will soon crack.

Surfaces	Glossy Alkyd Paint	Glossy Latex Paint	Flat Alkyd Paint	Flat Latex Paint	Latex Shingle Paint	Alkyd Shingle Paint	Rubber-base Paint	Cement Paint
Raw Wood								
Wood, plywood, or clapboard	✔		✔	✔				
Particle board	✔		✔					
Hardboard	✔	✔	✔	✔				
Rough wood siding			✔	✔	✔	✔		
Wood shakes and shingles			✔	✔	✔	✔		
Exterior wood trim	✔	✔						
Raw Masonry								
Plaster		✔		✔		✔		
Gypsum wallboard		✔		✔				
Concrete		✔		✔			✔	✔
Cinder block		✔		✔			✔	✔
Brick		✔		✔			✔	✔
Stucco	✔	✔	✔				✔	✔
Ceramic tile or glass								
Bare Metal								
Steel or iron	✔							
Galvanized metal								
Aluminum	✔	✔	✔	✔				
Copper or bronze								
Previous Surface Covering								
Wallpaper		✔	✔	✔				
Flat alkyd paint or primer	✔		✔			✔		
Flat latex paint or primer		✔		✔	✔		✔	
Alkyd glossy paint or varnish	✔		✔					
Glossy latex paint		✔		✔				
Epoxy paint or varnish	✔		✔					
Urethane paint or varnish	✔		✔					
Rubber-base paint	✔	✔	✔	✔			✔	
Cement paint								✔
Zinc-rich metal primer	✔	✔	✔	✔				
Aluminum paint	✔	✔	✔			✔		
Block filler	✔	✔	✔	✔			✔	✔
Wood filler	✔		✔			✔		
Wood preservative	✔		✔			✔		
Masonry sealer	✔	✔	✔	✔			✔	✔

EPOXY PAINT	URETHANE PAINT	PORCH AND FLOOR PAINT	MARINE PAINT	MULTICOLOR PAINT	LATEX SAND PAINT	LATEX TEXTURE PAINT	DRIPLESS PAINT	FIRE-RETARDANT PAINT	ALKYD VARNISH	EPOXY VARNISH	URETHANE VARNISH	SPAR VARNISH	ALKYD STAIN	EXTERIOR LATEX STAIN	ALKYD PRIMER	LATEX PRIMER	ALKYD CEMENT PRIMER	ZINC-RICH METAL PRIMER	ALUMINUM PAINT	WOOD SEALER	MASONRY SEALER	SILICONE WATER REPELLENT	BLOCK FILLER	WOOD FILLER	WOOD PRESERVATIVE
✔	✔	✔	✔				✔	✔	✔	✔	✔	✔	✔	✔	✔	✔			✔	✔				✔	✔
	✔		✔				✔	✔	✔		✔	✔	✔	✔	✔	✔			✔	✔				✔	✔
✔	✔	✔	✔		✔	✔	✔	✔	✔		✔	✔			✔	✔			✔	✔					
													✔	✔	✔	✔			✔		✔				✔
													✔	✔	✔				✔		✔				✔
	✔		✔					✔	✔	✔	✔	✔	✔	✔	✔				✔		✔			✔	✔
				✔	✔	✔		✔					✔	✔						✔					
				✔	✔	✔		✔							✔										
✔	✔	✔		✔	✔	✔		✔					✔	✔						✔			✔		
	✔			✔	✔	✔		✔					✔	✔						✔			✔		
✔		✔		✔	✔	✔		✔		✔			✔	✔						✔			✔		
				✔	✔	✔		✔					✔	✔						✔			✔		
✔			✔						✔	✔															
✔			✔						✔				✔	✔	✔	✔	✔								
													✔	✔	✔	✔									
✔	✔								✔				✔	✔		✔	✔								
✔	✔		✔						✔				✔			✔		✔							
				✔											✔	✔									
	✔	✔	✔				✔	✔	✔		✔				✔	✔			✔						
	✔	✔		✔	✔	✔	✔				✔				✔	✔									
	✔	✔	✔				✔	✔	✔		✔				✔	✔			✔						
	✔	✔		✔	✔	✔	✔				✔				✔	✔									
✔		✔	✔					✔																	
	✔	✔								✔															
		✔					✔																		
	✔	✔																✔	✔						
	✔	✔					✔	✔											✔						
✔	✔	✔		✔	✔	✔		✔							✔							✔	✔		
✔	✔	✔	✔					✔		✔	✔	✔	✔		✔									✔	
	✔							✔		✔	✔	✔	✔		✔				✔						
	✔			✔	✔	✔		✔													✔				

SELECTING A COATING—INTERIOR

Here and on the pages that follow, the interior coatings listed in the chart on pages 116 to 117 are discussed in detail. They are grouped in three categories: finishing paints; primers, sealers, and fillers; and special finishes.

Finishing Paints: After color, gloss is the most important factor in choosing a finishing paint. The four gloss types available are high gloss, semigloss, low sheen (or eggshell), and flat. High-gloss paints are the most wear-resistant because they contain a great deal of resin, the ingredient that solidifies into the coating film. The more resin, the tougher the film. This toughness makes glossy paints ideal for areas subject to heavy use or frequent washing—particularly kitchens and bathrooms. Semigloss and low-sheen paints afford moderate durability with a less obtrusive shine for most woodwork. Flat paints provide a desirable low-glare finish for surfaces that do not need frequent washing.

Primers, Sealers, and Fillers: If a surface is incompatible with the paint you want to apply—or is too rough to yield a smooth finish—the solution is to first use an undercoat like a filler, sealer, or primer. Fillers smooth uneven or damaged wood surfaces, and sealers close the pores of wood or masonry. Most common of all undercoatings are primers, which serve as a bridge between a finishing coat and an incompatible surface. Primers always have a flat finish in order to provide the rough texture, or "tooth," needed for good topcoat adhesion.

Special Finishes: There are also a number of paints designed for special needs, like hiding a flaw in a wall or ceiling *(page 37)*. These paints usually cost more and are harder to use than conventional paints, but are often worth the time and expense.

FINISHING PAINTS

Latex Paint
SIMPLIFIES CLEANUP
VIRTUALLY ODOR FREE
QUICK DRYING

The most widely used covering for walls and ceilings, latex paint consists of plastic resins and pigments suspended in water. Having water as its solvent gives latex a number of advantages over other kinds of paints: Tools, spills, and hands can be cleaned with soap and water; it is nearly free of odor and harmful fumes; and a coat usually dries in little more than an hour.

Latex adheres well to most surfaces painted with flat oil or latex paint, but it does not adhere to some alkyds and tends to peel away from any high-gloss finish. It can be used over unprimed wallboard, bare masonry, and fresh plaster patches that have set but are not quite dry. Before applying it to new concrete, wash the surface with a 10 percent muriatic acid solution, then rinse it clean. (Always wear goggles and rubber gloves when using muriatic acid.) You can even paint over stain with latex, provided the stain does not have a topcoat of varnish. If it does, use alkyd paint instead *(right)*.

For all its advantages, latex also has drawbacks. Although it can be applied directly over wallpaper, the water in the paint may soak the paper off the wall. On raw wood, the water solvent swells the fibers, roughening the surface—a disadvantage where a smooth finish is desirable.

And if you apply it to bare steel, it rusts the metal.

Alkyd Paint
DURABLE
NEARLY ODORLESS

Made from organic solvents such as mineral spirits and synthetic resins called alkyds, these paints are more durable than latex paints. They are also quite versatile; many painted or wallpapered surfaces—and even bare wood—can be covered with alkyds. They do not, however, adhere to bare masonry or plaster, and should not be used on bare wallboard because they raise the nap on the wallboard's paper covering. Most alkyds are dry enough for a second coat in 4 to 6 hours.

Latex paints will not bond well to alkyd paints, but most other paints can be applied over them. If you plan to spread a new coat of alkyd paint over an old one, make sure that the solvent in the new paint is not any stronger than mineral spirits; a stronger solvent may dissolve the old paint and lift it off the surface. Alkyd paints are best for painting over varnish, though you must first wash the varnish with a strong detergent and then sand it so that the new paint will stick.

While alkyd paints have traditionally had a strong smell, recent formulations are nearly odor free. But keep in mind that alkyd fumes and the organic thinners used for cleanup are toxic and highly flammable whether you can smell them or not. For this reason, use alkyds only in well-ventilated areas and wear gloves while painting.

Rubber-Base Paint
GOOD FOR MASONRY
MOISTUREPROOF
FAST DRYING

This waterproof coating, made from liquefied rubber, is excellent for masonry, especially concrete basement floors. Prepare bare brick to accept this paint by sealing it with clear varnish, and new concrete by washing it with a 10 percent muriatic acid solution. (Wear goggles and rubber gloves when you are working with muriatic acid.)

Rubber-base paint is far more durable than latex, but it is only available in flat and low-gloss finishes and a narrow range of colors. It is also expensive, has a strong smell, and needs special solvents. But its durability, water-resistance, and quick drying time—a coat normally dries in an hour—make it an excellent choice for high-traffic, moisture-prone areas.

Cement Paint
RENEWS MASONRY
APPLY TO DAMP WALLS

This inexpensive coating gives a facelift to brick, stucco, or concrete by adding a thin layer of cement to the old masonry. Some types also act to retard water seepage—an advantage in basements. To get the best results, be sure to work the paint into every pore and crevice with a rough-surface applicator specially made for painting masonry (page 65).

Though some manufacturers make ready-mixed formulations, cement paint is also available as a powder, which is a mixture of white Portland cement, pigment, and often a small amount of water repellent. This powder is mixed with water just before use. To help the cement set, the wall must be kept moist during the job and for at least 48 hours thereafter. Tools and spills must be rinsed off before the paint sets.

Cement paint forms a poor base for all other finishes.

Epoxy and Urethane Paints
VERY DURABLE
TRICKY TO USE

These coverings, referred to collectively as plastic paints, are exceptionally elastic and resistant to abrasion, grease, dirt, and most chemicals. Although they are expensive, they are often the best covering for surfaces subject to chemical and physical stress—like floors, stairs, and the walls of kitchens and bathrooms.

In some respects the two types of paint differ. Urethanes can be used on bare wood or over latex, alkyd, or oil paint. Epoxies produce a slick, impervious coating on nonporous materials such as ceramic or metal tile, glass, porcelain, or fiberglass; they can also be used on concrete or wood floors, but they will not adhere to latex, alkyd, or oil paint.

The most durable plastics are two-part paints, which must be mixed just before use because they dry and harden rapidly. Both types require special solvents, which are listed on

the package labels, for cleanup.

Alkyd paints can be used over an epoxy or urethane, but the surface must be roughened first by sanding, to provide a coarse texture onto which the paint can adhere.

PRIMERS, SEALERS, AND FILLERS

Latex Primer
QUICK DRYING
ODOR FREE
EASY TO CLEAN UP

This water-base primer is especially valuable in preparing bare plaster, concrete, gypsum wallboard, or cinder block. Such masonry contains alkalis that destroy alkyd finishing coats; the latex primer forms a barrier between the alkalis and the finish. In addition, this primer serves as a bridge between incompatible types of paint, since almost all paints will adhere to it and it will adhere to almost any surface—even to glossy oil paint if you sand it first. You can use latex primers on raw wood, though they will roughen the grain.

A latex primer has many of the advantages of latex paint: it is virtually odor free, it dries in 2 to 4 hours, and cleaning up requires only soap and water.

Alkyd Primer
BEST UNDERCOAT FOR WOOD
GOOD BASE FOR ALL PAINTS
NOT RECOMMENDED FOR WALLBOARD

This type of primer is the best undercoat for raw wood, because it does not raise the wood grain. Some alkyd primers are also compatible with masonry, though it is a poor first coat on gypsum wallboard because alkyd raises a slight nap on the wallboard's paper covering. Most finishing coats —including all types of latex paint— adhere well to an alkyd base coat. Alkyd primers take overnight to dry; tools and spills can be cleaned with the solvents used for alkyd paints.

Metal Primer and Paint
PREVENT PEELING AND RUST

The most commonly painted metals are steel and aluminum. Steel must be kept painted or it will rust. And while aluminum does not rust, it eventually pits if left uncoated or exposed to harsh weather. There are two ways to cover either type of metal: you can use a metal primer followed by a finishing coat of paint, or a single coat of metal paint that acts as its own primer.

If you choose the former, the best primer for steel is an alkyd type that contains zinc, which rustproofs the metal. This formulation also works well for aluminum, or you can apply epoxy or urethane finishes directly to the bare metal as self-primers. Any compatible finish can then be applied over these primers. The only exception is for painting a radiator; in this case, use only flat paint because glossy finishes trap heat.

In metal paints, primer and top coat are combined in a single mixture. These latex or alkyd paints come in high-gloss and semigloss versions and are available in a wide range of colors. They are applied by brush, and cleaned and thinned with the conventional solvents used for alkyd coatings.

All metal primers and paints must be applied to a surface that is absolutely free of dirt, grease, and corrosion. Before painting the metal, clean off grease with paint thinner. If there are any rust spots, either remove them or seal them with rust-onverting sealer *(page 54)*.

Copper, brass, and bronze hardware are not normally painted. Instead, the fixtures are usually lacquered at the factory to preserve their original appearance. If the lacquer wears away unevenly, first clean the finish off completely with a lacquer remover. Then, in the case of copper and brass, remove tarnish with fine steel wool and metal polish—or, for a mirror finish, metal polish alone—and apply a protective coating of polyurethane or epoxy varnish. Uncoated bronze develops an attractive patina that you can protect with varnish; if you prefer bright bronze, treat it like brass. To paint over these metals, use an alkyd metal primer containing zinc and any compatible finishing paint.

Sealers and Primer-Sealers
SEAL PORES OF WOOD AND MASONRY
PRESERVE NATURAL LOOK OF WOOD

These liquids, made of synthetic resins mixed with a high proportion of solvent, seal the pores of wood and masonry.

Transparent wood sealers sink into the wood's pores, binding the fibers together and making them easier to sand. They protect wood against dirt and moisture, and seal in the natural dyes and resins that can seep through paint. They dry more rapidly than most primers and do not alter the appearance of the wood. Stain, varnish, and alkyd paints may be brushed directly over a clear wood sealer, since sealed wood can still absorb liquid.

Masonry sealers—often tinted a translucent blue to make it easier to see the areas that have been coated—are used on concrete, cinder block, or plaster to prevent chalking. They also slow the passage of water through basement walls. Masonry sealers vary greatly in their composition; consult the label of the package for cleanup instructions and for compatible topcoats if you intend to paint over them.

Wood Filler
SMOOTHS WOOD
CAN BE MIXED WITH STAIN

A combination of synthetic resins and wood-toned pigment, wood filler is used to plug holes and build up rough or damaged sections in wood. It is available in either paste or liquid form. The paste type is usually thinned with a small amount of turpentine (or with a special solvent recommended by the manufacturer) and used to repair open-grain woods such as walnut, ash, oak, or mahogany. Liquid filler, which is simply a prethinned paste, is generally applied to woods with a closer grain, such as maple or birch. Neither the paste nor the liquid protect the wood; you must cover the filler with a coat of sealer and, in a surface subject to heavy use, a final coat of shellac, varnish, or paint.

You can repair minor damage in an already-painted piece of wood by patching it with paste filler colored with stain to match the wood finish.

SPECIAL FINISHES

Multicolor Paint
DISGUISES FLAWS
DISTINCTIVE AND DECORATIVE
These latex-base coatings contain two nonmixing pigments. Depending on the formulation, they produce either a tonal variation or a flecked appearance ideal for concealing uneven or slightly damaged surfaces. For indoor use, choose a brand that can be brushed or rolled on and does not require spraying. Any alkyd or latex paint can be applied over a multicolor paint, but two coats may be needed to hide it.

Sand and Texture Paints
DISGUISE FLAWS
YIELD ATTRACTIVE, ROUGH FINISH
DIFFICULT TO PAINT OVER
These paints give walls and ceilings a coarse texture that, like multicolor paint, conceals surface flaws. Sand paint is simply regular latex paint mixed with sand or a sandlike synthetic. It creates a fine-grained, glare-free texture that is attractive on ceilings but has a grittiness that limits its use to areas not likely to be touched. Texture paint is an extra-dense flat latex or alkyd paint. You can apply it as you would conventional paint to get a stuccolike finish, or follow the instructions on page 37 to get a deeply stippled finish.

These paints can be applied to surfaces compatible with their latex or alkyd base. The latex type is often used on wallboard ceilings, since it adheres without a primer and helps conceal the wallboard seams. Painting over them, however, presents special difficulties: you will need as much as 25 percent more paint than usual, and the rough texture will always show through the new coat.

Dripless Paint
GOOD FOR CEILINGS
EXPENSIVE
Formulated so thick that it does not drip from a brush or roller, dripless paint is an ideal finish for ceilings and other high, hard-to-reach places. It will usually cover any surface in a single coat, but it is considerably more expensive than conventional alkyds and covers less area per gallon.

Though dripless, this paint will spatter if it is carelessly applied, and its thickness makes it more difficult to clean up.

Fire-Retardant Paint
A WORTHWHILE PROTECTION
This paint slows the spread of fire by puffing up into a foamy, insulating layer when exposed to high temperatures. It is especially valuable in garages and basements, where many house fires start.

Be sure to follow the manufacturer's instructions when painting, especially in controlling the thickness of the coating: if it is too thin, it will not provide adequate protection; too thick, and it may fall away in case of a fire. And since the puffing ingredients in some types of fire-retardant paint remain water soluble even after the paint dries, check the label for cleaning instructions.

Available in latex flat and semigloss finishes, as well as in both urethane and epoxy formulations, fire-retardant paints can be applied over any surface that is suitable for latex. You can also cover bare wood with it, provided a perfectly smooth finish is not essential. But you should never apply conventional paints over fire-retardant paint, because they impair its effectiveness.

Outdoor paints suffer great extremes of temperature and moisture and are often applied to rough surfaces, so they must be both elastic and weather resistant. They contain more plasticizers—agents that promote flexibility—and frequently have a high proportion of resin, which acts as a binder to hold the various ingredients together.

How long a properly applied paint job lasts depends largely on when you think it begins to look drab and dull. Bright colors fade faster than others, and stains and varnishes yellow somewhat after a few years.

When possible, match new paint to old, latex on latex or alkyd on alkyd. Never apply alkyd over latex, but you can repaint alkyd with latex—if you begin with an alkyd-base primer. Use this method when you don't know the formulation of existing paint or if you want to switch from alkyd to latex for greater mildew resistance. The primer will stick well to either and provides a good foundation for a latex top coat.

In addition to providing little nourishment for mildew, latex paints retain color longer than alkyd paints. Latex is thinned and cleaned up with water, making it more convenient than alkyd, which requires solvents such as mineral spirits for thinning and cleaning.

Stains, which contain a lower proportion of pigment to resin and solvent, come in clear, semitransparent, and opaque varieties. They allow the natural texture of house siding to show through while still protecting the surface. Some stains are available in either latex or alkyd bases.

Varnishes and other clear coatings rarely last as long as paint because ultraviolet rays in sunlight penetrate them and alter the character of the surface they cover. Such changes reduce the bond between surface and finish—sometimes in less than 2 years. However, a clear finish with ingredients to block ultraviolet radiation, called UV absorbers, will last longer.

Primers, preservatives, and sealers provide raw wood, metal, or masonry with extra protection against moisture and form a base when a surface and the desired top coat are incompatible.

FINISHING PAINT

Latex flat
LOW ODOR
BEST FOR HUMID CONDITIONS

Latex flat, also called low-luster, is a popular choice for most exterior siding surfaces because it dries faster than alkyd paint. It also allows water vapor to escape through the paint from underneath rather than expanding into a blister. This ability to "breathe" makes latex a good choice for a damp exterior wall. Like its interior counterpart, latex can be used on masonry, but remove as much chalking as possible before painting. If the old surface is still chalking heavily, latex paint may not adhere perfectly or, if it holds at first, may not prove quite as durable as an alkyd-base paint.

Alkyd flat
BEST FOR CHALKING SURFACES

Alkyd exterior paints adhere and cover all surfaces well except latex and unprimed masonry or metal. On damp surfaces alkyd paint may blister and peel more easily than latex, but alkyd adheres to chalking surfaces better than most water-thinned paints.

Gloss and semigloss trim
MORE WASHABLE THAN FLAT

Glossy paints contain more resin than flat paints, which gives them greater resistance to wear and washing and makes them best for window and door trim, doors, and shutters. Their shiny finish, however, makes glossy paints more likely to show surface imperfections than flat paints. Both alkyd and latex exterior glossy paints wear well and are available in high gloss and semigloss finishes, although alkyd high gloss is slightly less shiny than its latex counterpart. Because latex gloss dries faster than alkyd, it is preferred for getting doors and windows back into service quickly. Latex is also more weather and alkali resistant than alkyd paint.

Marine paint
VERY DURABLE
EXPENSIVE

These glossy paints contain more epoxy, urethane, acrylic, or alkyd resins in proportion to their pigment content than ordinary exterior finishing paints. This added resin increases durability—marine paints were originally designed to protect boats against salt water and bruising weather. Their excellent wearing qualities have made them popular for outdoor wood or metal house trim, although they are expensive.

Porch and floor paint
HIGHLY ABRASION RESISTANT
FOR CONCRETE OR WOOD

Formulated to withstand bad weather and traffic on concrete porches and outside steps, these alkyd and latex paints resist abrasion but are prone to chalking and fading, especially when exposed to extreme temperature variations. Before any floor paint is applied to new concrete, the surface must be carefully prepared to provide "tooth" (page 61). Latex floor paint can then be applied directly to the concrete, but with an alkyd floor paint, you must prime the surface, either by thinning the paint itself according to the manufacturer's specifications, or with one of the primers listed opposite.

Glossy alkyd and latex paints can be used on bare or previously painted wood floors or on previously painted masonry floors.

Shingle paint
POROUS TO LET WOOD BREATHE

For an opaque finish on houses sided with shingles, use special flat shingle paints, available in latex and alkyd bases. These permit moisture to escape from behind shingles, where it can accumulate in damp weather. By allowing shingles to "breathe" as water vapor escapes, these paints help prevent wood rot and paint blisters. Latex shingle paints work equally well on bare or most previously coated wood shingles.

Metal paint

USED DIRECTLY ON METAL

METALLIC OR COLORFUL FINISH

Metal paints stop rust to greater or lesser degrees and are thinned with mineral-spirit solvents. Aluminum paint (powdered aluminum that is suspended in alkyd resin) provides a shiny, metallic finish and is particularly durable. It is suitable for most primed metals.

Glossy alkyd-base metal paints are available in an assortment of colors and are easy to use since no primer coat is required. Before applying most of these paints, be sure to clean and prepare the surfaces *(page 59)*.

Some of these alkyd-base metal paints contain penetrating, rustproofing agents and can be applied directly to rusty metal. Even with these so-called rustproofing paints, however, it is advisable to remove all rust and dirt before applying the coating.

Masonry paint

LATEX EASIEST TO USE

Not all masonry paints are waterproof or intended for exterior use. Read the manufacturer's directions carefully. These paints come in latex and special alkyd bases, although latex is generally recommended for exterior cinder block because it allows moisture to pass through.

Masonry surfaces must be properly prepared before painting *(page 61)*, and as much chalk as possible must be removed. If exterior masonry is chalking heavily, first use a block filler *(far right)* or a masonry sealer *(page 120)*.

STAINS AND CLEAR FINISHES

Stains

PROTECTIVE MATTE FINISH

REQUIRE MIXING

Exterior stains, because they are thinner than paint and penetrate rather than coat wood, are ideal for rough wood siding and shingles because they easily reach all the small nooks and crannies of these coarse surfaces. No primer is needed with stains, which range from nearly transparent to opaque. Exterior stains contain more pigment than interior stains and so must be mixed like paint before use. Water-base latex stains resist wear and retain their color longer than alkyd-base stains. Latex stains also breathe well and are preferred in damp conditions that might cause an alkyd finish to blister. Opaque stains last nearly as long as many paints.

Varnish

URETHANE TYPE IS TOUGHEST

SPAR VARNISH BEST NEAR SEASHORE

Exterior varnish is used exclusively on wood—to protect it from weathering while retaining the natural appearance and color. No exterior varnish lasts as long as an interior one; most have a life expectancy of no more than 1 or 2 years. To prevent yellowing, a good quality exterior varnish contains ingredients called UV absorbers.

The most commonly used varnish is spar varnish, which must be renewed every 12 to 16 months. Although it provides excellent protection against salt corrosion if kept in good condition, under most other circumstances, alkyd-base exterior varnish lasts slightly longer. Acrylic varnishes are intended for ornamental metal.

PRIMERS, PRESERVATIVES, AND SEALERS

Primers

EXTRA FLEXIBLE

A SPECIAL TYPE FOR GALVANIZED STEEL

Exterior primers are extra flexible to adjust to wall expansion and contraction caused by changes in the weather. Otherwise, these undercoats are essentially the same as those used inside the house *(pages 119-120)*. A special kind of alkyd-base primer that contains Portland cement protects exterior steel. Since it has a zinc additive, it can be used on galvanized metal gutters and drains.

Wood preservative

PROTECTS AGAINST INSECTS AND FUNGI

USED ONLY ON BARE WOOD

Raw wood exterior surfaces can be protected against insect and fungus damage with clear or tinted wood preservatives. Some waterproof varieties deter boards from warping on a deck or porch. Do not apply a wood preservative to surfaces that have been stained or painted; they must penetrate the wood to work. Unless painted, clear preservatives should be replenished every year, tinted varieties every 2 or 3 years.

Block filler

A MASONRY SEALER

AN UNDERCOAT FOR PAINT

Rough and porous masonry surfaces can be sealed and smoothed by these thick, white coatings that provide a good base for latex- or alkyd-base finishes. Block filler can be applied with a paint roller, but a rough-surface applicator *(page 65)* is more effective.

Silicone water repellent

A BARRIER TO ALL OTHER COATINGS

PRESERVES WOOD AND MASONRY

These nearly invisible coatings reduce to a minimum water seepage through exterior wood surfaces. The silicone repels all paint finishes for several years, so this preservative should be used only to maintain the original appearance of the wood. Some types of water repellents use paraffin wax instead of silicone. These must be replenished every year to maintain water protection. Water repellents are available in clear and tinted varieties.

CHOOSING A WALL COVERING

This chart provides wall-covering information essential to achieving satisfactory results. Wall coverings are sold in single-, double-, or triple-length rolls in various widths.

Some wall coverings benefit from a foundation of lining paper, an inexpensive, unpatterned paper pasted to the wall in advance of the patterned covering. Lining paper speeds drying of adhesive after the final wall covering is hung, and it provides an exceptionally smooth base on rough walls for any type of wallpaper. Coat the wall with primer-sealer *(page 72)* before hanging lining paper. Use an undiluted heavy-duty vinyl adhesive for the lining paper, and hang the strips either horizontally or vertically; if vertically, stagger the seams between lining paper and patterned paper. Leave $\frac{1}{8}$-inch gaps around obstacles, between strips, and along ceilings and baseboards to allow for a direct bond between final paper and wall. Coat the lining paper with the same primer-sealer, then use the recommended adhesive for the final covering. When hanging a wall covering in a bathroom or other high-moisture area, add a mildew-inhibiting agent to the paste.

Some coverings are described as "scrubbable," others as "washable." There are no industry-wide definitions for either of these terms, so follow carefully the manufacturer's recommendations for cleaning. If you no longer have them, experiment in an inconspicuous spot to confirm that your cleaning agent doesn't discolor the wall covering and to see how vigorously you can rub the surface without damaging it.

Type	How Sold
Common Papers Untreated Vinyl-coated Strippable	Single, double, and triple rolls, 18 to 27 inches wide; length and width combine to provide 28 to 30 square feet per single roll, yielding about 25 square feet after waste allowance
Vinyls Laminated to paper Laminated to woven fabric Impregnated cloth on paper backing Laminated to unwoven fabric	Same as common papers; heaviest grades also available in widths to 54 inches and lengths to 30 yards
Foils Simulated metallic Aluminum laminated to paper Aluminum laminated to cloth	Same as common papers
Flocks On paper On vinyl On foil	Same as common papers
Prepasted Coverings Papers Vinyls Foils Flocks	Same as common papers
Fabrics Untreated Laminated to paper Self-adhesive	Bolts range from 36 to 45 inches wide, but also available in widths of 54 and 60 inches; sold by the yard
Textured Coverings Grass cloth Shiki silk Hemp Burlap	Double rolls, 36 inches wide and 24 feet long, except burlap, which also is available in widths to 54 inches
Laminated Wood Veneers Random patterns Matched veneers	Strips 10 to 24 inches wide and up to 12 feet long; end-matched strips for taller walls available on request from manufacturer
Gypsum-Coated Wall Fabric	Single rolls, 48 inches wide and 30 yards long

Adhesives	Handling Hints	Special Comments
Premixed cellulose paste or vinyl adhesive	Follow basic procedures (pages 80-95); treat carefully to avoid rips	Susceptible to grease stains and abrasions; pattern inks may run if washed
Mildew-resistant type; vinyl adhesive suggested	Does not stick to itself; double-cut all overlaps (page 89)	Most durable type currently available; may be scrubbed; almost always strippable
Mildew-resistant type; vinyl adhesive suggested. Check manufacturer's recommendation	Hang over lining paper to minimize wall defects; avoid wrinkles, which cannot be smoothed	Fragile and hard to handle; may cause glare in sunny areas; available in striking supergraphics
Same as for corresponding unflocked paper, vinyl, or foil, but slightly thicker	Vacuum loose flock particles before applying adhesive; hang over lining paper to ensure smooth surface	Might be damaged by excessive rubbing
Water-activated, applied at factory. Some use a special activator solution instead of water	Use water box (page 81); follow manufacturer's instructions for soaking	Ideal for the inexperienced paperhanger
Powdered vinyl adhesive or double-faced vinyl tape if fabric is untreated; stainless cellulose paste or lightweight vinyl adhesive if laminated	Paint all woodwork before hanging; hang over lining paper; stretch fabric until taut but not out of shape	Vacuum to clean
Premixed cellulose paste or vinyl adhesive	Reverse every other strip top for bottom to prevent abrupt changes of shading; avoid excess moisture, which causes fibers to separate from backing; hang over lining paper for faster drying	All available in either natural or synthetic fibers; Shiki silk, a fine grass-cloth type, also sold in overprinted designs
Specified by manufacturer	Set room temperature to 70°F or higher for fast drying; use manufacturer's recommended sequence when hanging matched veneers	Fire-resistant; allowed by strictest city codes where solid wood paneling is banned
Supplied by manufacturer	Set room temperature to 70°F or higher for fast drying; reverse every other strip, top for bottom	Dries to plasterlike surface; available only in limited shades, but may be painted in other colors

INDEX

Time-Life Books is a division of Time Life Inc.

PRESIDENT and CEO: John M. Fahey Jr.

TIME-LIFE BOOKS

MANAGING EDITOR: Roberta Conlan

Director of Design: Michael Hentges
Director of Editorial Operations:
  Ellen Robling
Director of Photography and Research:
  John Conrad Weiser
Senior Editors: Russell B. Adams Jr.,
  Dale M. Brown, Janet Cave, Lee Hassig,
  Robert Somerville, Henry Woodhead
Special Projects Editor: Rita
  Thievon Mullin
Director of Technology: Eileen Bradley
Library: Louise D. Forstall

PRESIDENT: John D. Hall

Vice President, Director of Marketing:
  Nancy K. Jones
*Vice President, Director of New Product
  Development:* Neil Kagan
*Associate Director, New Product
  Development:* Elizabeth D. Ward
*Marketing Director, New Product
  Development:* Wendy A. Foster
Vice President, Book Production:
  Marjann Caldwell
Production Manager: Marlene Zack
Quality Assurance Manager: James King

HOME REPAIR AND IMPROVEMENT

SERIES EDITOR: Lee Hassig
Administrative Editor: Barbara Levitt

Editorial Staff for *Paint and Wallpaper*
Senior Art Director: Cynthia Richardson
Picture Editor: Catherine Chase Tyson
Text Editor: Denise Dersin
Associate Editors/Research-Writing:
  Mark Galan, Tom Neven
Technical Art Assistant: Angela Miner
Senior Copyeditor: Juli Duncan
Copyeditor: Judith Klein
Picture Coordinator: Paige Henke
Editorial Assistant: Amy S. Crutchfield

Special Contributors: John Drummond
  (illustration); Jennifer Gearhart, William
  Graves, Craig Hower, Marvin Shultz,
  Eileen Wentland (digital illustration);
  George Constable, Peter Pocock (text);
  Mel Ingber (index).

Correspondents: Christine Hinze (London),
  Christina Lieberman (New York), Maria
  Vincenza Aloisi (Paris).

PICTURE CREDITS

Cover: Photograph, Renée Comet. Art,
Carol Hilliard/Totally Incorporated.

Illustrators: Adolph E. Brotman, Nick Fasciano, Elsie J. Hennig, Walter Hilmers Jr.,
Fred Holz, Peter McGinn, Ray Skibinski,
Vantage Art, Inc., Whitman Studio, Inc.

Photographers: (Credits from left to right
are separated by semicolons; from top to
bottom by dashes.) **End papers:** Renée
Comet. **10:** Werner Ladder Company.
11: Louisville Ladder Corporation,
Louisville, Ky. **12, 13, 22, 31, 32, 35:**
Renée Comet. **37:** Renée Comet;
William Zinsser & Company (3). **46, 47:**
Renée Comet. **48:** Diana Adams; Kenneth Rice. **49:** Alan Briere; Robert
Finken/The Picture Cube—Kenneth Rice.
50: Kenneth Rice—Aneal Vohra/Unicorn
Stock Photos—Kenneth Rice. **51:**
George White Jr.; Doug Adams/Unicorn
Stock Photos—Kenneth Rice. **57, 66,
70, 71, 74:** Renée Comet.

ACKNOWLEDGMENTS

Joseph Biber, Dutch Boy Paints, Cleveland;
Jeanne Byington, Sumner, Rider & Associates, New York.; Ken Charbonneau, Benjamin Moore Paints, Montvale, N.J.; Rob
Cooksey, Louisville Ladder Corporation,
Louisville, Ky.; Esther del Rosario, Silver
Spring, Md.; Kimberly A. Fantaci, National
Guild of Professional Paperhangers, Dayton; Jeff Fantozzi, Western Wood Products
Association, Portland, Oreg.; Debra Fedasiuk, William Zinsser & Company, Somerset, N.J.; Teri Flotron, National Decorating
Products Association, St. Louis; Marcy
Graham, F. Schumacher & Company, New
York; Frank Granelli, William Zinsser &
Company, Somerset, N.J.; Steve Harman,
DAP, Inc., Dayton; Tony Hedgepeth, Fairfax, Va.; Martin Kobsik, Werner Ladder
Company, Greenville, Pa.; Joseph Koppi,
Koppi Communications, West St. Paul,
Minn.; Frank Magdits, Benjamin Moore
Paints, Montvale, N.J.; Doug Mingst,
Northeast Industries, Midland Park, N.J.;
Ruth Pestorius, Decorating with Paint,
McLean, Va.; Wagner Consumer Products
Division, Minneapolis; Shelley Walk, Dutch
Boy Paints, Cleveland; Rick Watson, Duron
Paints, Beltsville, Md.; Diane Wood,
William Zinsser & Company, Somerset,
N.J.; Murphy Wright, A & A Rental Station,
Alexandria, Va.

First printing. Printed in U.S.A.
Published simultaneously in Canada.
School and library distribution by Time-Life
Education, P.O. Box 85026, Richmond,
Virginia 23285-5026.

TIME-LIFE is a trademark of Time Warner
Inc. U.S.A.

**Library of Congress
Cataloging-in-Publication Data**
Paint and wallpaper/ by the editors of
  Time-Life Books.
p. cm. — (Home repair and improvement)
Includes index.
ISBN 0-7835-3896-0
1. House painting. 2. Paperhanging.
I. Time-Life Books. II. Series.
TT320.P25 1995
698'.142—dc20   95-30729